Fly-Fishing in France

With

Phil Pembroke

Fly-Fishing in France
Author – Phil Pembroke
Copyright Philip Pembroke 2006
Published by Phil Pembroke 2007
ISBN - 978095469276

CONTENTS

	Page no		Page no
		Maps	
Introduction	1		
A-Z of fly-fishing in France	2	Calvados	13
		Blavet River	51
Licences and regulations	3	Couesnon River	56
Salmon and trout in France	6	Gouët River	60
		Jarlot River	67
Calvados	12	Penzé River	69
Morbihan	50	Quimper area	72
Ille-Et-Vilaine	55	Steir River	75
Cotes D'Armor	59	Odet River	78
Finistère	66	Corrèze	83
Quimper area	72	Lozère	102
Corrèze	82	Ariège	139
Lozère	101		
Ariège	138		
Fish of the Pyrenees	169		
More fishing books	172		
Conclusion	174		
Glossary 1 –salmon conservation bodies in France	174		

Northern France is a popular holiday destination for visitors from the UK. Brittany for instance contains one third of the French coastline into which flow thousands of fish filled rivers. The cuisine is excellent as are the wines, the weather is not too hot and the fishing is guaranteed to bring a smile to all who visit.

In 1944 allied soldiers after the Normandy landings fought their fiercest battles in the Bocage region. Today the river Touques in the département of Calvados provides some of the finest sea trout angling sport in Europe.

The neighbouring region of Brittany offers the best salmon fishing in France including the Scorff River situated in Finistère. Lozère département near the Auvergne in central France is one full day's drive from Calais it has wonderful trout fishing along the scenic Tarn gorges. As does nearby Corrèze dspartement on the wonderful Vezère River in the region of Limousin.

Ariége is located in the south of France on the border with Spain it is a prime destination for those anglers hoping to catch some of France's famous mountain lake fish e.g. the cristivomer a ferocious lake predator. Visitors in summer should be prepared to brave towering Pyrenean passes where the only option in many cases for stocking fish in these beautiful but remote glacial tarns is by helicopter.

In France anglers can fish for as little as €30 for trout and salmon when they purchase the Carte de Pêche Vacances – holiday fishing licence in wonderful lakes and rivers for any two week period during the summer months. In Brittany the holiday licence is available all year.

This represents great value when one considers that some anglers fishing one day on a river beat in Scotland will often be charged hundreds of pounds for the pleasure. If not thousands: for one week of fishing.

Anglers intending to visit France are reminded that a free copy of the Guide de Pêche booklet can be obtained by contacting the angling federation of the region they intend to visit – details for these federations are provided under chapter heading. It is also available from local bars and shops that sell the angling licence and tourist offices. This free booklet gives accurate and up to date information on the latest rules and regulations for rivers and lakes to fish in each département. As well as updates to carp night fishing areas where changes might occur.

A-Z OF FLY-FISHING IN FRANCE

Fish species (*-introduced species)

- Corégone* – Common whitefish / Swiss char
- Huchon* - Huchen salmon
- Omble chevalier/arctique – Arctic charr
- Omble de fontaine*- American Brook charr
- Omble du Canada/ Cristivomer * – American Lake charr
- Ombre commun – grayling
- Saumon royal * – Chinook salmon
- Saumon argenté * – Coho salmon
- Saumon fontaine*- brook trout
- Truites autochtones – wild brown trout
- Triute fario– brown trout
- Truite arc-en-ciel* - rainbow trout
- Truite brune de mer – sea trout

Useful words

- Ascenseur – fish elevator
- Barrage – dam and reservoir behind it
- Bombette – ledgering
- Bredouille – fishless
- Buldo – bubble float with fly droppers
- Castillon – small salmon, spending one year at sea
- Cuiller tournante – spinner
- Écluse – lock
- Empoissonnements – fish stocking
- Hameçon sans ardillon – barbless hooks
- Lancer - spinning
- Leurres; vairon – minnow lure, poissons nageurs - spinners, cuillères tournantes – revolving spoons, ondulantes - wobblers
- Lisse - run
- Mouche – fly
- Mouche artificielle fouettée – fly-fishing
- Mouche fouettée – artificial fly lures
- Mouche noyée – wet fly.
- Parcour – stretch of river
- Parcours de pêche –fishing stretch often stocked
- Parcours sans tuer – catch and release fishing stretch

- ❖ Pisciculture – fish farm
- ❖ Plans d'eau – artificial lake
- ❖ Poisson nageu – spinning lure
- ❖ Raider – fast powerful river stretch
- ❖ Ruisseau – stream / brook
- ❖ Ultra-light- light spinning with a minnow lure or spinner

ANGLING LICENCES AND REGULATIONS

The Carte de Pêche is the French angling licence However France is famous for its bureaucratic tradition *un imbroglio juridique* and when it comes to fishing regulations they don't disappoint. The number of different types of licence available almost makes one feel sorry for the pêcheur Francais. Luckily the visitor is spared its worst excesses.

This is what you do. Most anglers from the U.K. will purchase the Carte de Pêche Vacances. This allows fishing for a 15 consecutive day period in lakes and rivers of both 1st and 2nd categories, usually from June to September. It can be obtained from tackle shops, local bars, Décathlon national sports chain where English is spoken, Mondial Pêche and Europêche chains, and regional angling associations. Remember to take along a passport photo and I.D. If no French is spoken present a photo of your self, holding a fish and they will get the idea.

The Carte Journalière is a day ticket it is usually available only for the summer months but often available all year. Under 16's qualify for the Carte Jeune, which is usually half price. Under 12's often go for free but are still obligated to obtain a Carte de Pêche.

Outside the summer months an annual French angling licence - Carte de Pêche is required. What you must ask for is a Carte de Pêche avec la taxe complète this allows fishing in both 1st and 2nd category waters for all fish species.

A Carte de Pêche avec taxe complète – angling licence, including the stamp that indicates that you have paid the Taxe Piscicole - French rod licence tax for one département area will cost you approx. 55 - 65 euros and entitles you to fish all of the public lakes and rivers within that département and throughout France. Essentially half the cost of the Carte de Pêche the Taxe Piscicole goes to the national angling body in Paris called the APPMA.

The APPMA stands for the Association pour la Pêche et la Protection du Milieu Aquatique. They are the national angling body.

For more information contact:	Union Nationale pour la Pêche en France et la Protection du Milieu Aquatique, 17 Rue Bergère - 75009 Paris Tel. 0148249600 - Fax. 0148010065 E-mail: union.peche@unpf.fr
Or the French Fly-Fishing Federation	Fédération Française des Pêcheurs à la Mouche et au Lancer, 73 Quai Auguste Deshaies - 94854 IvryCedex, Tél. 01 45 21 01 69, Fax. 01 46 71 25 59 Email: SIEGE.FFPSML.FR@wanadoo.fr http://www.ffpml.com/accueil.htm

Anglers can also buy reciprocal stamps that allow you to fish the public waters in all the bordering départements. These cost just a little more. It is recommended that you buy this additional stamp as it opens up the fishing in more than half the départements in France. It is called the Entent Haliautique et Grand Ouest This entitles you to fish no less than 55 other départements throughout southern, central and northwest France.

The annual Carte de pêche is valid for public areas for everyone, some private water, and local angling club waters that often are often open to the public. Visitors may fish private water but are often required to purchase local day tickets or a local season ticket for longer periods. This is because privately managed waters do not always offer reciprocity with the départemental angling licence.

Waters are again, divided into 1st category waters for trout and salmon fishing. But: not exclusively. Fishing for zander, pike, perch in France known as carnisseurs – predatory fish also requires a Carte de Pêche Complète – 1st category licence.

2nd category waters are for coarse fishing. In general the trout season runs from 13th March to 19th September. The coarse season is all year. The exceptions are pike and zander - carnisseurs fishing in 1st and 2nd category waters where a close season operates in spring and is stated for each region.

Angling licences are available in France from département angling federations, Décathlon and Mondial Pêche sports outlet chains. Local bars, restaurants, tackle shops and tourist offices. Details are given under each chapter heading.

Salmon and trout production in France

90 % of the salmon consumed in France come from farming. Imports of salmon range from 120,000 to 130,000 tons per year. Almost 35 % of the consumption is dedicated to smoked salmon now affordable for most consumers. 18,000 tons are produced domestically, of which 15 % is exported.

In the early 1980's France starting rainbow trout and coho salmon farming. The coho salmon *Oncorbynchus tkisutch,* known as saumon argenté in France comes from the North Pacific Ocean.

A recreational angler fishing from St. Peter Port harbour Guernsey on July 21, 1977 caught a coho salmon. It weighed 681 grams and had presumably escaped from a fish farm.

Coho production never picked up and its production ceased, due to the fragility of the species during the first summer at sea and the need to produce juveniles for its development.

In France, despite the fact that salmon is the most widely consumed fish, there is a low production of Atlantic salmon - 460 tons at sea in 2003 in two marine sites in Normandy and Brittany. There is limited development of fish farms along the French coastline, due to a lack of offshore sites, despite a well-proven technology.

The objective is to produce more than 3,000 tons. In fresh water, juveniles are produced in the South-West of France for sea farming, repopulating, and preservation of at least two strains of the species; another full cycle production site is located in Brittany

The future for wild salmon in France

Atlantic salmon – *salmo salar*, known in France as Saunon atlantique is a magnificent fish, it used to migrate up all the major West European rivers, from the North of Portugal to the Arctic Circle. By the 1980's, they had disappeared from all big rivers in France, except the Loire and its main tributary the Allier.

This makes the Loire-Allier salmon a unique fish in Europe: it is the only salmon species to pocess the qualities necessary for an 800 km migration between the Loire estuary and its spawning grounds. And is now the last genetic stock of large wild salmon that has recently been used for reintroducing the species on other large rivers in France and Europe for instance the Rhine, Garonne and Dordogne.

On the estuary of the Loire River, at the end of the 19th century, about 10,000 salmon that is an estimated 100 tons, used to be taken every year. On the upper Allier, before the Saint-Etienne du Vigan dam was built, the villages of Luc, Langogne and La Bastide used to export about 10 tons of salmon (approximately 1,000 fish) to the South of France. Early in the century, anglers used to come from all over Europe to Brioude to catch salmon on the Allier River.

Dams are considered the main reason for decline in fish stocks. There used to be about 100,000 salmon on the Loire-Allier basin. By 1990 there were only a few adults left: in the autumn of 1996, 67 adult salmon used the salmon elevator at the Poutès-Monistrol dam to go and breed on their spawning grounds on the upper Allier. The collapse of salmon catches - from 30,000 to 45,000 in 1890 to less than 1,000 catches since 1975 is due to dams, first built for navigation purposes in the 19th century, then for hydroelectricity. They have blocked the way to salmon's natural breeding areas and are located al lalong the Loire River.

On the Allier River, the EDF (the Electricity Generating Authority of France) dam of Saint-Etienne du Vigan (built in 1895, dismanteld in 1998) has been closing off for a century about 50 hectares of the best upper basin spawning grounds, while the Poutès-Monistrol dam (built in 1941) has totally stopped all migration for half a century, until a salmon elevator was built in 1986. From 1941 to 1986, only 8% of the 2,200 hectares of breeding areas used in the early 19th century were accessible. As for the Allier's main tributaries the Sioule, Dore, Allagnon, and Chapeauroux, they have all been almost sterilized.

The upper Loire, the access of which became difficult in 1845 when the Decize navigation dam was built, became totally closed to salmon when the Grangent (1957) and Villerest (1983) dams were built. On the Vienne-Creuse-Gartempe basin, migration is still blocked by the EDF dam of Maisons-Rouges (dismanteld in 1998): salmon disappeared from the Vienne River in 1930, while the Cher River - another tributary of the Loire was steriliz as early as 1858.

Apart from dams, salmon must face other problems: silting up and salinization of the Loire estuary, varied obstacles for instance nuclear plants and bridges, dredging for gravel heating up of the water engendered by nuclear plants, excessive fishing, and pollution. The measures launched by the Plan Grandeur Loire Nature attempt to improve the situation.

The Atlantic salmon's journey

Born in the clear waters of the upper basins, young salmon grow up in their birthplace during a period that spans from 1 to 3 years on the Allier River. On the last spring of this period, they undergo a phenomenon called smoltification, which will turn them from freshwater fish into saltwater fish. Juveniles, now called smolts, descend the river to the Atlantic to their feeding grounds. They stay off the coasts of Greenland and the Feroe Islands 1 to 4 summers, feeding on shrimps and little fish, gaining 2 to 3 kilos a year. Then, moved by breeding instinct which lead them back without fail to their native river, they begin their 6,000 km overall, 900 km upstream the river, journey back.

As they enter the river, salmon must negotiate more than than 20 major dams. Nowadays, salmon need more than 6 months to reach their spawning grounds; it used to be 2 months when the river had no dams. When they enter the Loire river mouth, Atlantic salmon are a slender silver fish, with a shining metal-like coat. Their size and weight vary greatly, according to the number of years they spent at sea: generally, they weigh between 5 to 10 kilos and are 70 to 90 cm long. When they reach the spawning grounds where they were born to finally breed, they are worn-out and wasted by a fast which has been lasting for 6 to 14 months according to the date they entered the estuary; they weigh no more than half or two thirds of their original weight.

Activity peaks in April for big salmon that spend 1 to 3 years at sea, and June-July for salmon that spend 1 year at sea called castillons. Spawning occurs in December and fry occur in March. After 1-2 years smolt return to sea.

Launched in January 1994, the Plan Loire Grandeur Nature aimed at reconciling economic development, flood control environment protection on the Loire basin. It plans notably several measures aiming at restoring the populations of Loire-Allier migratory fish: salmon, the most symbolic migratory species, but also eel, sea trout, shad and lamprey. Indeed, salmon are not the only fish migrating up the Loire and the Allier rivers. Sturgeon sadly disappeared in the early 1930s.

The Plan Loire Grandeur Nature required the demolition of two EDF dams (Saint-Etienne du Vigan on the Upper Allier and Maisons-Rouges on the Vienne River) and the improvement of about 10 obstacles, notably in 1996 and 1997, the nuclear plants' sills. The construction of a fish ladder on the dam-bridge of Vichy is now finished.

The goal on the Allier basin is to give back to salmon about 300 hectares of spawning grounds, notably on its tributaries the Sioule, the Dore and the Allagnon Rivers. On the Vienne basin, which used to represent a fourth of the Loire basin salmon spawning grounds in the 19th century, part of the breeding areas have already been rehabilitated; the demolition of the Maisons-Rouges dam will enable salmon to recolonize the Creuse and Gartempe rivers.

Salmon are such an endangered species that two additional measures have been launched. Adults still naturally come and breed on the Upper Allier, but they are so few that all fishing has been banned for at least 5 years and a large hatchery was built at Chanteuges on the upper Allier, in the département of the Haute-Loire. The objective ws that by 2004 6,000 adults would show up in the estuary every year. €1,240,000 were spent on the new salmon hatchery for the Haut-Allier designed to produce 2 million fish eggs annually. The same amount again is set aside for construction of counting stations and fish ladders. Half the budget is paid for with E.U. grants.

But there is stil work to be done. On the Upper Allier, nothing is planned for the demolition of the old EDF Poutès-Monistrol dam. On the Upper Loire, the Villerest and Grangent dams are not equipped with fish ladders. As for the Loire estuary, a crucial passage during the migration, it is threatened by the extension of the Saint-Nazaire port and the construction of a new nuclear plant.

For more information see www.saumondeloire.com
Email: sosloirevivante@rivernet.org

More contact addresses for salmon cosevation NGO's are given at the end of the guidebook.

Has the salmon restoration plan succeeded?

At the time the Plan Loire Grandeur Nature initiated in 1994 was regarded as Europe's largest salmon campaign. The plan's objective was to produce 2,250,000 fish eggs in the first year with a return on the adult spawning grounds of 1,200 salmon within 5 years and to double the second generation. In 2000, the cameras installed on the fish pass of the barrage De Vichy recorded only 377 salmon returning.

However the aim was to produce quality above quantity and the loading of the spawning grounds was 8-10 times less than in a commercial fish farm. The number of adult salmons recorded ascending in 2001 was slightly higher at 400 in Vichy on the Allier River basin and at least 7 in Châteauponsac on the Gartempe River basin. The plan was failing.

In 2002 the salmon was facing extinction from the Loire-Allier River basin. There were believed to be roughly 200-300 fish left. The Salmon Life project was formed to rejuvenate this unique salmon population. In 2002 salmon were released into the Allier, Sioule and Gartempe Rivers at a cost of €1.5 million.

Approximately 220,000 parr (juvenile salmon) were released at 16 points along the Allier and Gartempe Rivers from where they began their 1000 km journey to the sea. On the Allier River basin there were roughly 175.000 parr released in spring 2002: 150,00 in the Allier River itself between Prades and Brioude in département Haute-Loire and 25,000 in the Sioule River between Châteauneuf-les-Bains and the Pont de Menat located in Puy de Dôme. The parr were reared at the Augerolles salmon hatchery from the spring of 2001 and continued their growth at Chanteuges fish farm.

In addition 44,000 parr were released by the federal fish farms at Talbat (Vienne) and Verger (Creuse) on the Gartempe River downstream of Châteauponsac in the departments of Vienne and Haute Vienne. The larger fish will start their migration to the sea from March to April. The smaller fish will stay in fresh water for another year. The fish will stay at sea for three years before returning.

The fish elevator at Golfech on the Garonne River recorded an increase in salmon returning to spawn. 599 salmon were counted in December 2002. In Tuilière on the Dordogne River 1022 salmon and 304 sea trout were counted. On the Adour River 167 salmon were caught with rod and line in 2001, but 800 salmon were caught in nets in the estuary. It is commercial fishing that is considered the primary threat to salmon stocks and an issue the authorities hope to tackle next.

The salmon-angling scene in France

Access to salmon angling is considered more democratic in France than in the UK where priviledged anglers pay in excess of £4000 for one week fishing on the Test River. A survey from 2001 has proved both encouraging and worrying. 2,761 anglers purchased the timbre migrateur required for catching salmon but this angling licence also includes sea trout. This is less than in 1987 when the Allier was closed to salmon anglers but up over the past ten seasons by 23%.

2,244 salmon were rod caught in 2000. Representing four fish caught for every five anglers. The average number of salmon caught per angler is less than one unit, down from just over one unit from 1994-1996. Fishing logbooks show that 43% of anglers blanked. In Normandy the average time it takes an angler to catch one salmon is 94 hours. Previously it was in excess of 150 hours.

The improvement has been due to the extension of the season for one-year old salmon called castillons into the summer. It takes an angler twice as much time to catch the more highly prized spring salmon. These are the mature breeding fish most at risk and for which quota limits have been introduced to conserve their stocks.

Where quotas have been implemented on the Sée, Léguer, Sélune and Douron Rivers stocks have increased. However as a whole there are insufficient spring salmon returning to French Rivers to sustain a viable population. However where salmon fishing is banned on the Dordogne and Garonne Rivers numbers have increased significantly.

CALVADOS 14

For more information contact: Fédération pour la Pêche du Calvados
18 rue de la Girafe - 14000 Caen
Tel, 02 31 44 63 00
Fax, 02 31 44 81 63
Email: peche.calvados@wanadoo.fr

For more help contact: Le Comité Départemental du
Tourisme du Calvados
8 rue Renoir, 14054 Caen cedex 4,
France Tel, 0231279030
Fax, 0231279035
www.calvados-tourisme.com
Email: cdt@cg14.fr

Calvados is famous for its apple brandy. No visitor to this département should leave without having tried one glass. Nor should any angler hesitate to investigate some of France's best trout and sea trout waters found in Normandy.

Most of the rivers in Calvados contain trout. The areas of Virois and Bocage situated in the west of the département support the highest density of wild brown trout in a complex network of streams and brooks. In summer grasshopper or worm is the choice of bait of traditional local anglers. But for the native brown trout spinner or fly lures work best in the smaller channels.

There are 6 river basins in the Calvados département, they are the Aure, Orne, Dives, Seulles, Touques and the Vire.

The chalk streams situated to the east produce larger fish. Catching them is possible using a minnow lure cast downstream under an overhanging branch. Fly fishermen often achieve success by using a large emergent mayfly lure then later on in the season turn to CDC fly lures.

Local fly-fishing club, Club Mouche Cormellois always welcomes visiting anglers. Their president Yvon Carbonne at Mairie chairs bi-monthly meetings held in Cormelles le Royal, rue des écoles 14123. Of interest is a new parcours de pêche – a new stretch of 2 km of riverbank

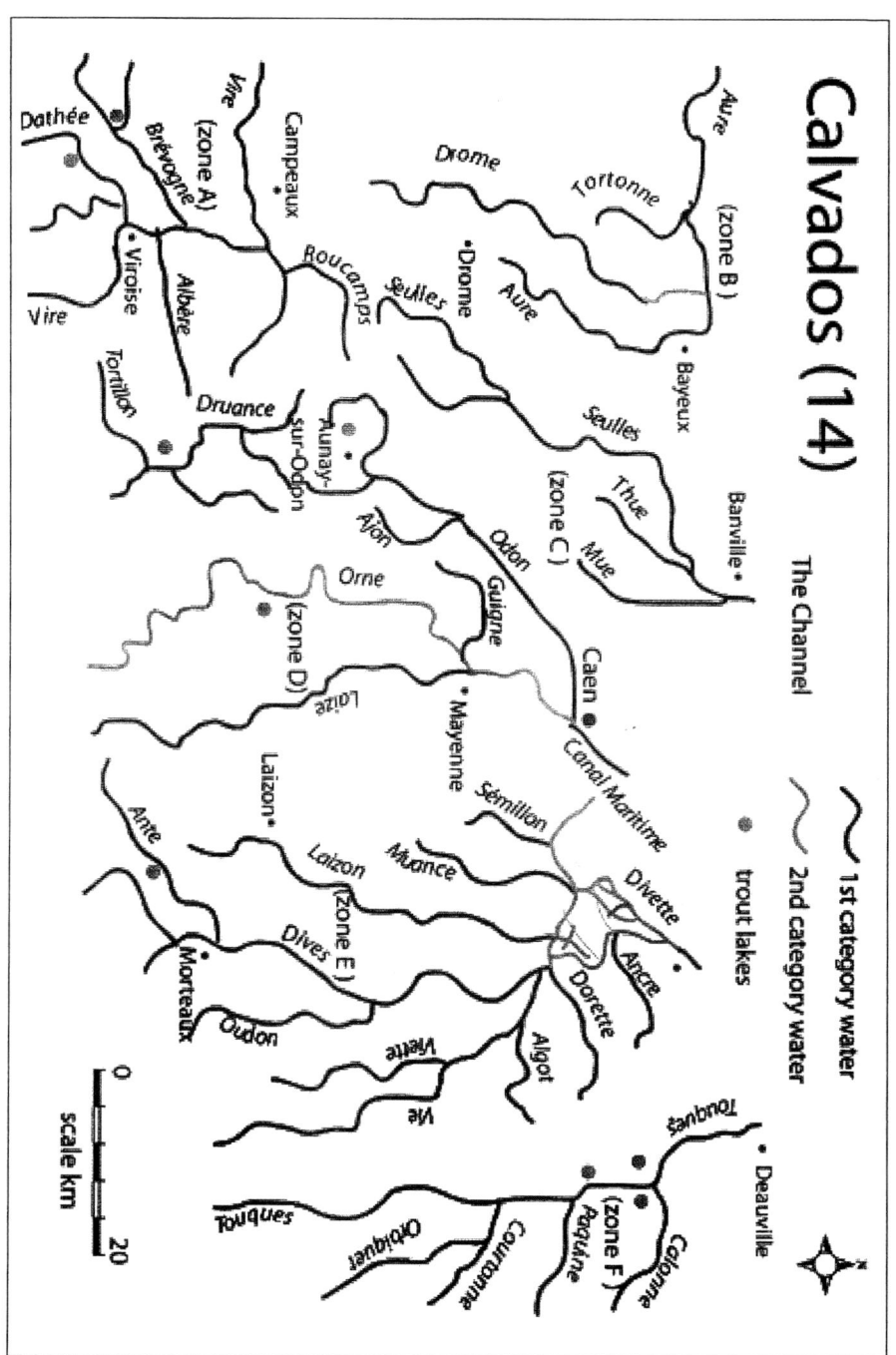

called L'ancre near Douville en Auge - D 45c where only fly-fishing is allowed. The angling club AAPPMA la Côte Normande manages it.

There are seven more fly-fishing parcours de pêche – fishing stretches they exist on the river Touques, and are managed by local angling club AAPPMA la Société de Pêche Lexovienne. See below for details.

Rules and regulations

The season for 1st category rivers and lakes is from the 2nd Saturday in March through September. From half an hour before daybreak: to half an hour after sunset.

Brown trout and saumon fontaine- brook trout may be fished for from the 2nd Saturday in March through to the 3rd Sunday in September. 23-25cm is the minimum caught size that can be bagged up but this figure depends on location.

Rainbow trout can be fished for from the 2nd Saturday in March through to the 3rd Sunday in September in water classified as sea trout. Fishing is allowed all year in 2nd category water.

Salmon fishing is prohibited in Calvados at present. But its reintroduction is taking place at present on the river Orne. Fishing for grayling is also not permitted.

Rivers and lakes where fishing takes place do not tolerate dogs.

Angling Licences

The Carte adulte avec taxe complète – permits fishing in 1st and 2nd category water. This is the annual fishing licence that you will require to fish for trout over any period more than two weeks.

On 1st category water – one rod and one line with not more than two hooks is permitted. When Spinning or fly-fishing no more than 3 fly lures are allowed, dead or live baiting are allowed.

(State whether river is stocked or left wild)

The Carte Jeunes is endorsed for those anglers less than 16 years of age. Holdars are permitted to fish in both 1st and 2nd category water they have the same rights as the Carte adult complète – full angling licence.

The Carte exonérés is for anglers less than 16 years of age and low-income groups. It permits fishing in 1st and 2nd category water with one rod and not more than two hooks, all methods of fishing are allowed except spinning (for predators).

The Carte découverte is available free of charge to anglers less than 13 years of age it permits fishing with a single pole but no fishing reel. No lures and live baiting are allowed

The Carte journalière is a day ticket, it permits all methods of fishing in 2nd category water and in the ponds and lakes that are classified as either 1st or 2nd category. Please request "une carte spécifique mouche à la journée" when you want a trout fishing day ticket.

The Carte vacances, holiday licence is valid for 15 consecutive days fishing from the 1st June through 30th September. All methods of fishing are allowed on both 1st and 2nd category water.

The Carte de Pêche annuelle d'une AAPPMA du Calvados – annual départemental angling licence for Calvados and Carte Vacances permits fishing in all areas classified as public water on the rivers Touques, Dives, Orne, and also on the parcours fédéraux.

Found below are sketch maps and brief descriptions of individual rivers and lakes that contain trout.

Zone A is found on the main départemental map

The local angling club that manages this area is called La Gaule Séverine, they can be contacted at: Rue de la Basse Fosse 14380 Saint Sever Tel, 0231688971 / 0231660985.

Saint Sever is situated 60km from the regional capital of Caen in the heart of the area known as Bocage.

Parcours de pêche are fishing stretches stocked regularly with trout managed by the AAPPMA local angling club

1st category water

River Sienne: fish from the barrage du Gast to the pont de la Prise at Beslon.

On the rivers Senène, Brevogne, Dathée and Drôme there are 41 km of rivers and brooks to choose from.

Into these waters 400 kg of brown trout (23-25 cm) are released before the season begins. 22,000 fry during the year. 30,000 trout eggs are released into local brooks every January.

Étang du Vieux Château de Saint-Sever, 2 ha in area: situated in the forêt domaniale de Saint Sever. Licences and day tickets are available from the Bar du Bocage and Bar le Mondial. The venue is closed on Friday. The lake supports brown and rainbow trout that are stocked weekly. Anglers here also enjoy catching pike, carp and eels.

Accommodation: Camping Municipal Saint Sever Tel, 0231688263 Gîtes ruraux Mairie de Saint Sever Tel, 0231688263.

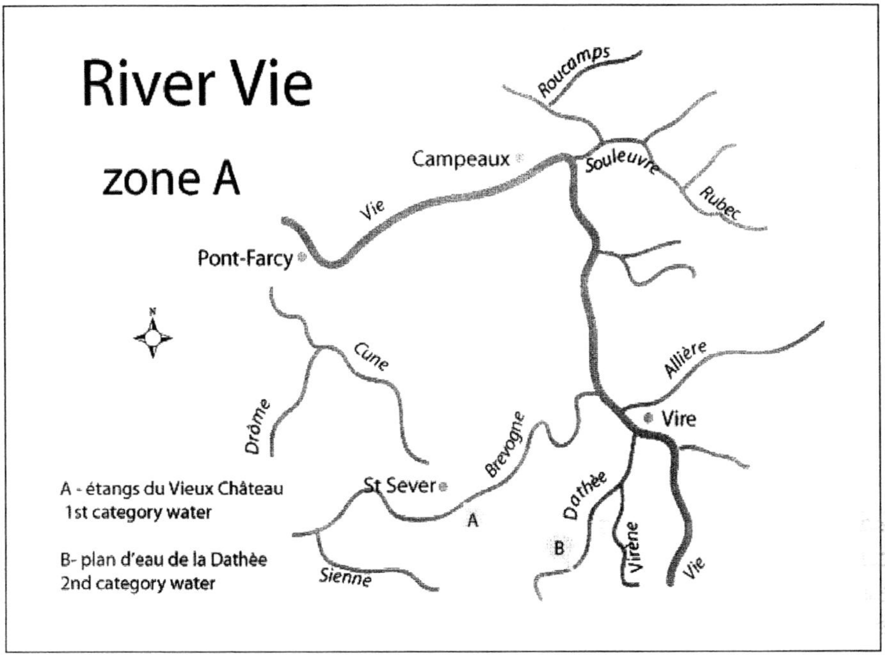

River Vie
zone A
Roucamps
Campeaux
Souleuvre
Rubec
Vie
Pont-Farcy
N
Cune
Drôme
Allière
Vire
Brevogne
A - étangs du Vieux Château
1st category water
B- plan d'eau de la Dathèe
2nd category water
St Sever
A
Dathèe
B
Virène
Vie
Sienne

Sant-Sever-Calvados
D 524
to Vire
Route
Forestiere
to
Fontenermont
D 81
La Clairère
to RD 293
étangs du Vieux
Château
to Le Gast

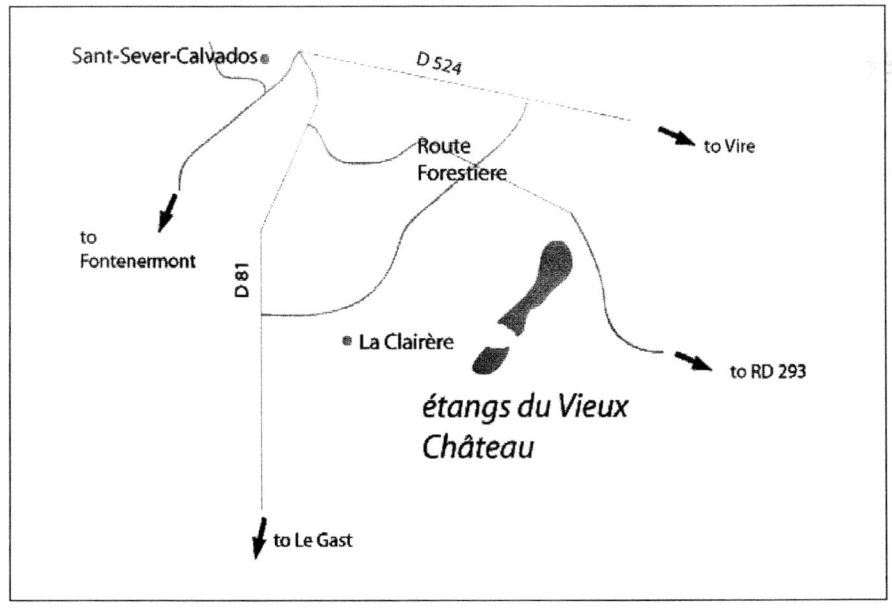

Licences and day tickets are available from: Bar Tabac, Le Bourg, 14380 Champ Du Boult Tel, 0231660283.
Other places to fish for trout in the Bocage

River Vire, fish upstream of the pont de Campeaux, rivers Dathée, Virène, Allière, Jourdan, Brévogne, Souleuvre, Crincelle, Roucamps, Courbançon, Drôme - right bank up to pont de Drôme, Cune, Sienne, la Glénon, Diane and Jouvine - until the pont de Clairfougères, Tortillon – until the pont de Soliers. You can also fish tributary and affluent streams where signposted.

No wading is allowed on these waters except from the pont d'Etouvy to the pont de Campeaux. A 10-bag limit applies.

Licences and day tickets are available from: Point Info Tourisme, square de la Résistance, 14500 Vire. Bar PMU Le Narval, rue Ancienne Poissonnerie, 14500 Vire.

An 8 km fishing stretch on the river Drôme exists from the pont de la Plumée up to the river Vire, domaine privé. Brown trout are caught here.
There is a 4 km stretch on the river Sottière.
And a 4 km stretch on the river Corbine.

A 6 km stretch exists on the river Cauquefourque from its source up to the confluence with the river Drôme. Because the water is classified as private it maintains no reciprocity with the rest of the region, invalidating the département fishing licence. Instead anglers will require a day ticket or local season ticket from this particular locality.

Brown trout.

4km stretch on the river Gouvette from the border of the département up to the river Vire, private water. Brown trout.

5km stretch on the river Coisel (le Tison) from its source until the river Vire, private water. Brown trout.

Accommodation: Camping Municipal Pont-Farcy Tel, 0231694612
Gîtes ruraux: Mairie de Pont-Farcy Tel, 0231688648.

River Vire: fish from pont Etouvy up to pont de Campeaux.
River Drôme: right bank fish up to the pont de Drôme and its tributaries.

Accommodation: Hôtel de la Poste Le Bény Bocage Tel, 0231686301 Le Castel Normand Le Bény Bocage Tel, 0231687603 Gîtes ruraux: Mairie de Campeaux Tel, 02 31 68 66 20 Gîtes de Pêche: La Maison de l'Ile Campeaux Tel, 0231827165 Gîte du Parc Campeaux Tel, 0231827165

Licences and day tickets are available from: Le Symbolic, Le Bourg 14350 Campeaux Tel, 0231686611.

Parcours Fédéraux are river stretches managed by the Fédération de Pêche du Calvados, they include.

The river Vie at Brévière has 450 m of fishing along the right bank.

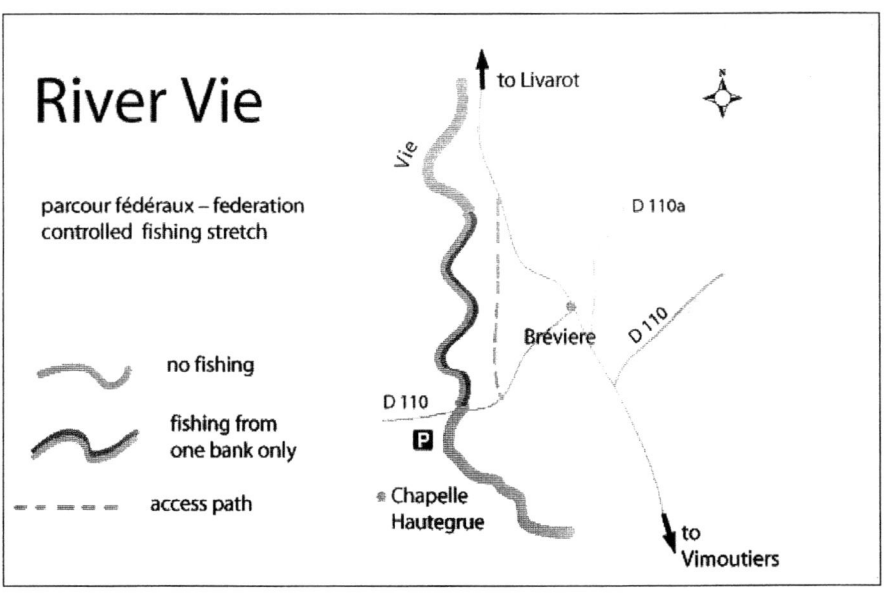

Zone B

The local angling club that manages this area is called Les Pêcheurs de la Drôme, they can be contacted at: Septs Vents, 14240 Caumont L'evente, Tel, 02 31 77 42 10.

Caumont L'Evente is situated 40 km from Caen.

Places to fish that are classified as 1st category water

River Drôme: upstream and downstream: fish from Bertherie, près - field de Dampierre towards Moulin de Bacon, town of Bazoque - maps IGN n° 1412 and 1413.

The river maintains 40 km of authorised fishing bank sign posted Pêcheurs de la Drôme. This is a river with a broad channel bed between 4 m and 10 m in width and a depth between 1 m and 2 m. The current flows quickly through this region of bocage - woodland, offering some very beautiful fly-fishing reserves found mainly on the central stretches.

Fish species that are present include mainly brown trout but there are some minnows and eels.

Fishing is permitted on Saturday, Sunday, Monday, Wednesday and public holidays. Spinning is permitted from the 1st April. The minimum size for bagged trout is 23cm with an 8-bag limit. Only hook size number 2 is permitted up to 1st April. No dogs are allowed.

Accommodation: Hôtel Saint Martin Caumont l'Eventé Tel, 02317751 60. Hôtel Saint Pierre Caumont l'Eventé Tel, 0231775022
Hôtel Le relais de la Forêt Montfiquet Balleroy Tel, 0131213978
Camping La Vallée de Craham Cahagnes Tel, 0231778818
Gîtes ruraux Mairie de Caumont l' Eventé Tel, 0231775029

Parcours de pêche – river fishing stretches

River Drôme – upstream stretches. Cassified as 1st category. Bordering the Département de la Manche.

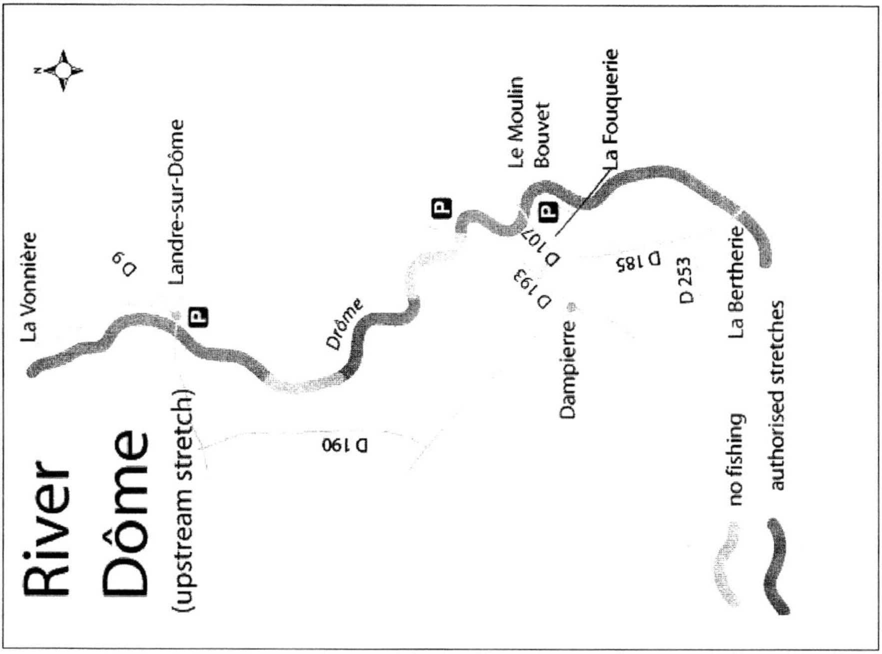

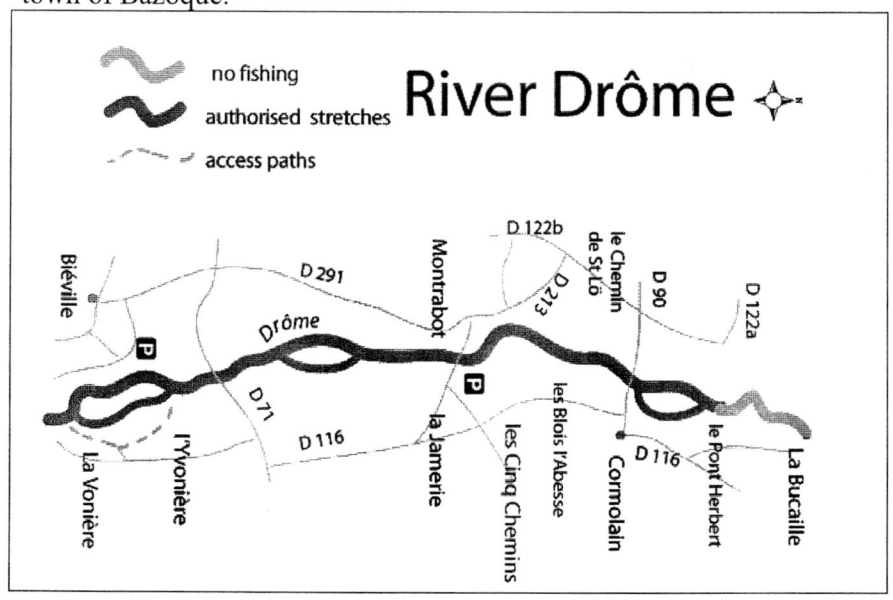

River Drôme: downstream stretches. 1st category. Bordering the département de la Manche. Upstream and downstream: fish from Bertherie, près de Dampierre towards the moulin de Bacon, situated by town of Bazoque.

Where do I purchase my angling licence and day tickets?

Café de Paris, Place du Marché14330 Le Molay Littry, Tel, 0231229537.Mondial Pêche, Rue Marcelin Berthelot, 14120 Mondeville, Tel, 02 31 83 00 20, fax, 02 31 83 00 40, Email: infos@mondial-peche.fr or visit: http://www.mondialpeche.fr

Zone D

The local angling club that manages this area is called L'Hameçon Versonnais, they can be contacted at: n° 14 Le Mesnil 14790 Verson, Tel, 0231781212 or 0231268540.

Parcours de Pêche: river Odon fishing stretches

Stretch 1. Louvigny. Fish from the start of the parcours de pêche until: the pont de Mesnil de Louvigny found further upstream. Fishing is allowed every day except occassional Fridays when restocking occurs. All artificial baits are allowed e.g spinning, deadbaiting and fly lures.

Stretch 2. Fish from: the pont de Mouen to the pont du Mesnil de Louvigny. In particular from: upstream of the pont du Mesnil de Louvigny until the Carrières de Mouen, please refer to the signs indicating the start and end of the fishing stretch.

Fishing is permitted on Monday, Wednesday, Saturday and public holidays. All artificial baits and lures are permitted. Minnow lures are allowed from 10th April. The fishing season ends on 17th September for this stretch.

Stretch 3. Upstream of the pont de Tourmauville until the pont de la route de Gavrus. Fishing is permitted everyday except occasional Fridays. All artificial baits are allowed from 10th April.

All three fishing stretches are closed by 17th September. The river is populated by brown trout some are wild brown trout and eels. 550 kg of brown and rainbow trout are released annually.

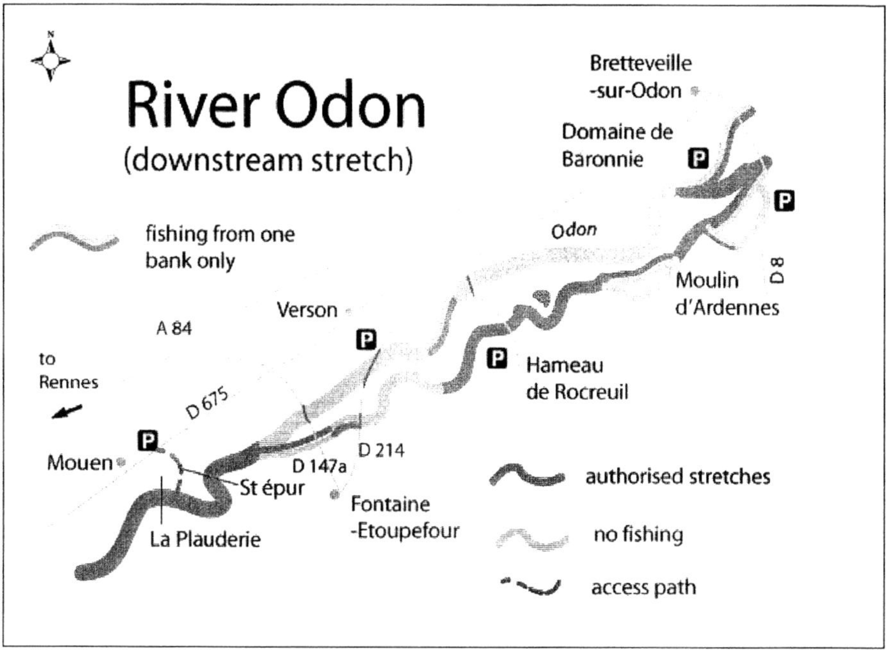

River Odon
(downstream stretch)

- Bretteveille-sur-Odon
- Domaine de Baronnie 🅿
- 🅿
- fishing from one bank only
- Odon
- Moulin d'Ardennes
- D 8
- Verson 🅿
- A 84
- 🅿 Hameau de Rocreuil
- to Rennes
- D 675
- Mouen 🅿
- D 214
- St épur
- D 147a
- Fontaine-Etoupefour
- La Plauderie

~ authorised stretches
~ no fishing
-~ access path

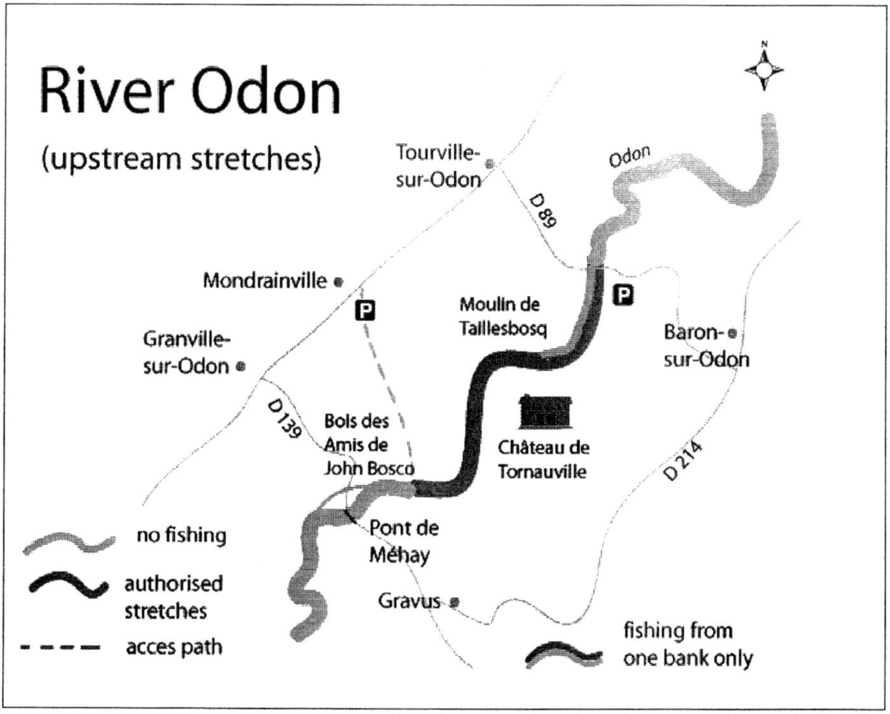

River Odon
(upstream stretches)

- Tourville-sur-Odon
- Odon
- D 89
- Mondrainville
- Moulin de Taillesbosq 🅿
- 🅿
- Baron-sur-Odon
- Granville-sur-Odon
- D 139
- Bois des Amis de John Bosco
- Château de Tornauville
- D 214
- Pont de Méhay
- Gravus
- fishing from one bank only

~ no fishing
~ authorised stretches
- - - acces path

23

Licences and day tickets are available from.

Bar Le Galopin, 2, place Pasteur, 14140 Livarot Tel, 02 31 63 54 67.
Office du Tourisme, 1, place Georges Bisson, 14140 Livarot Tel, 02 31 63 47 39.

The local angling club that manages this area is called La Guale Pétruvienne they can be contacted at: 52 route de Grisy, 14170 Saint Pierre Sur Dives Tel, 02 31 20 39 66/02 31 20 51 95.

Places to fish: river Dives from the pont de Vendeuvre to Ecajeul. Well signposted.

Fish present include trout, eels and poisson blanc - skimmers. Fishing is permitted on Saturday, Sunday, Wednesday and public holidays. And everyday after 13th May. No spinning is allowed till after 13th May. 8-bag limit, 25cm minimum size.

Recommended places to fish include by the Moulin d'Ouville and the site du Moulin de Carel.

Parcours de Pêche. River Dives: fishing stretch from Vendeuvre to Ecajeul.

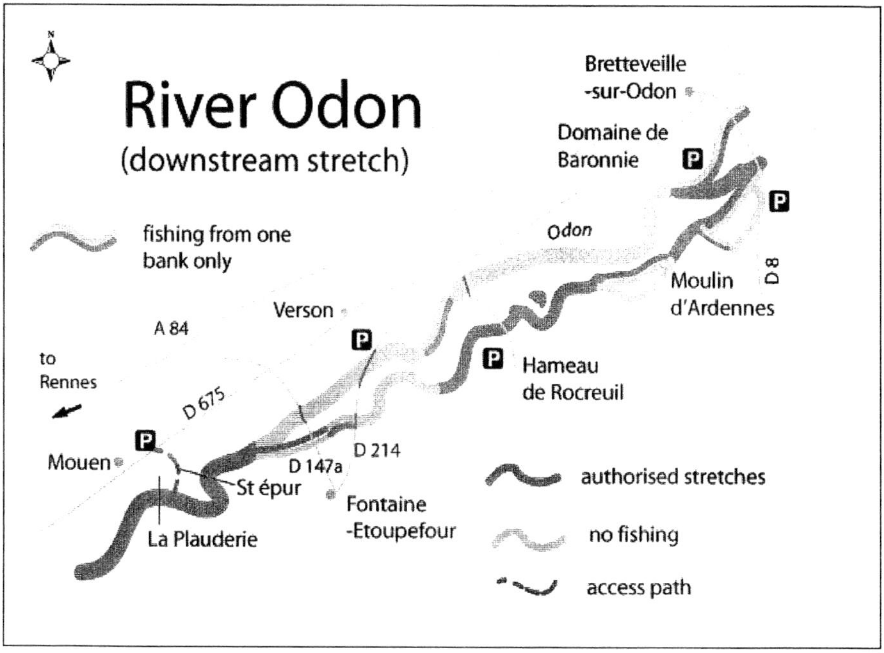

River Odon
(downstream stretch)

- fishing from one bank only
- to Rennes
- A 84
- D 675
- Mouen
- St épur
- La Plauderie
- Verson
- D 147a
- D 214
- Fontaine-Etoupefour
- Odon
- Bretteveille-sur-Odon
- Domaine de Baronnie
- Moulin d'Ardennes
- D 8
- Hameau de Rocreuil

Legend:
- authorised stretches
- no fishing
- access path

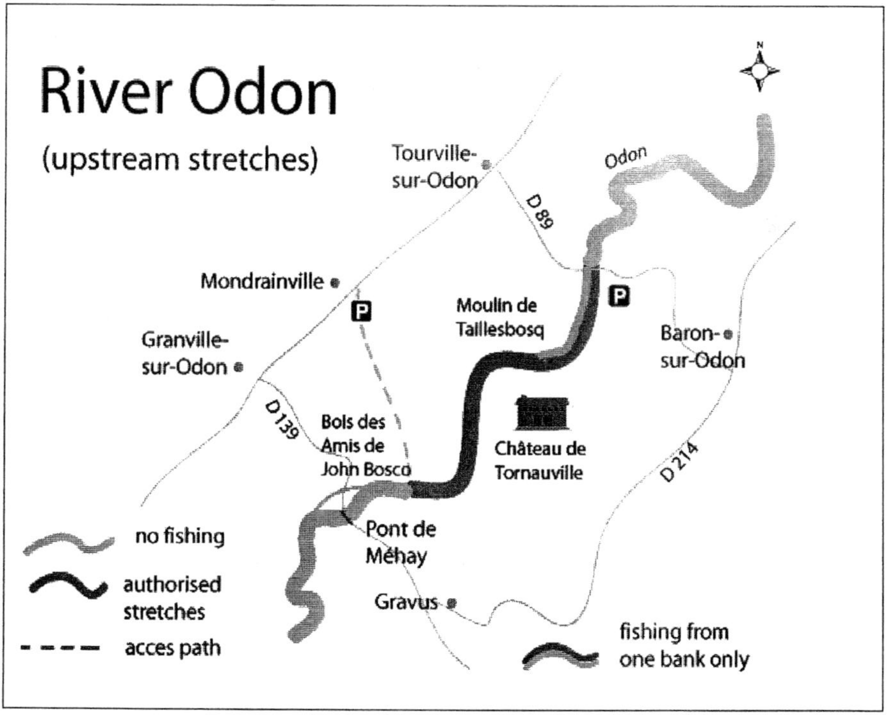

River Odon
(upstream stretches)

- Mondrainville
- Granville-sur-Odon
- D 139
- Bois des Amis de John Bosco
- Pont de Méhay
- Gravus
- Tourville-sur-Odon
- Moulin de Taillesbosq
- Château de Tornauville
- D 89
- Odon
- Baron-sur-Odon
- D 214
- fishing from one bank only

Legend:
- no fishing
- authorised stretches
- acces path

Licences and day tickets are available from:

La Pêche Sportive 140, rue d'Auge, 14000 Caen. Pêche Chasse, 12, rue Camille Blaisot, 14210 Evrecy Tel, 02 31 80 52 32.Tabac Journaux, 17, rue Guillaume le Conquérant, 14790 Fontaine Etoupefour Tel, 02 31 97 35 96.Le Bistrot, Route de Bretagne, 14790 Mouen Tel, 02 31 26 74 87.Libraire, rue du Général Leclerc, 14790 Verson

Zone D

The local angling club that manages this area is called La Truite Condéene, they can be contacted at: Mairie 14110 Condé sur Noireau Tel, 02 31 84 66 17/02 31 69 19 79.

Places to fish

70 km of river bank to fish from. Main courses are: river Druance, 25 km, from pont d'Escures at St-Jean-le-Blanc until Condé-sur-Noireau. River Noireau, 10 km of riverbank: from the pont de Caligny to the pont des Bordeaux. River Tortillon, 10 km of riverbank: from Vassy to Condé-sur-Noireau.

Streams: affluents of the river Druance include the Cresme, Halgré; affluents of the river Tortillon include the Ségande, Rocque, and Gourguesson. Anglers can fish all these streams

Plans d'eau: the barrage de Pontécoulant, plan d'eau du parc municipal de Condé-sur-Noireau. Anglers must be in pocession of the special Carte de Pêche journalière – day ticket categorised as journalière de la Truite, sold from the 1st April, annual trout angling licence held in this département or from neihbouring areas.

Trout are stocked at the start of the season on the rivers Druance, Noireau and Tortillon.

At Condé sur Noireau is found the parc municipal, 1st category water, no groundbaiting is allowed. One rod only.

At Pontécoulant, is found a lake called le barrage - dam, angling is allowed with two rods, during the trout season.

Parcours de Pêche – river stretches and lakes

Rivers Noireau, Druance, Tortillon and their tributaries, all of them are classified as 1st category. The retenue du barrage de Pontécoulant: and the plan d'eau municipal de Condé-sur-Noireau.

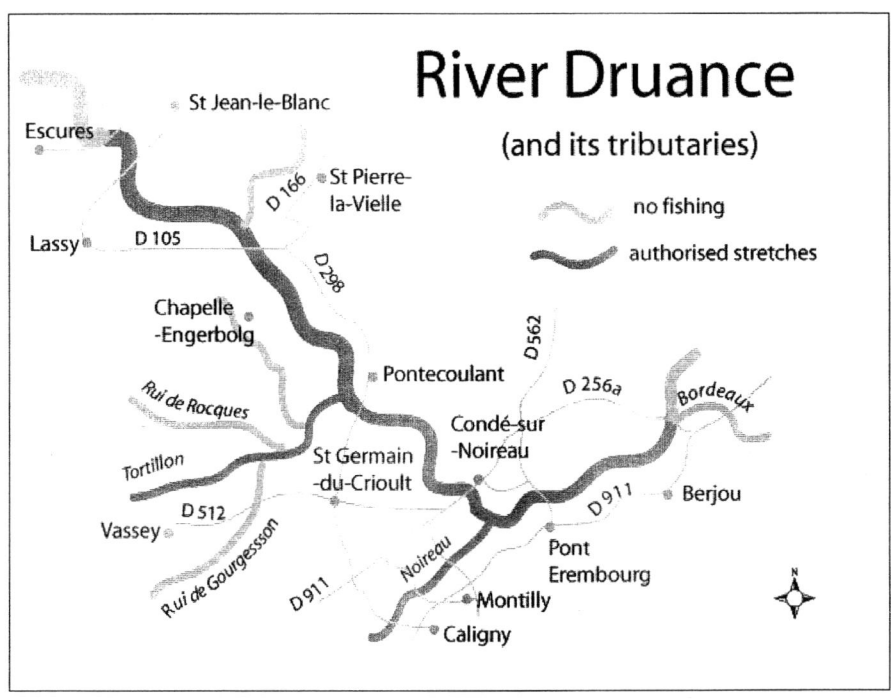

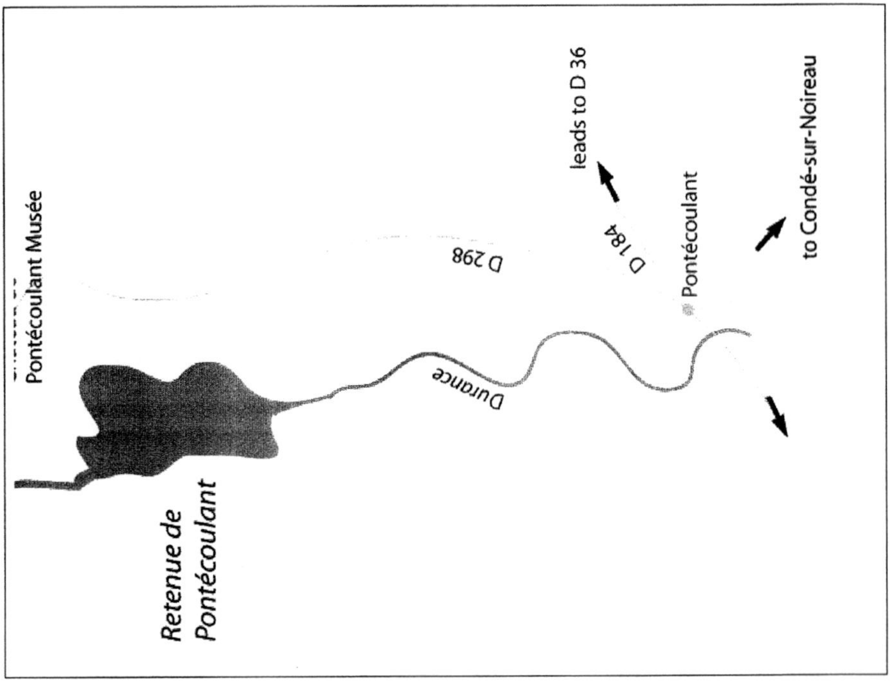

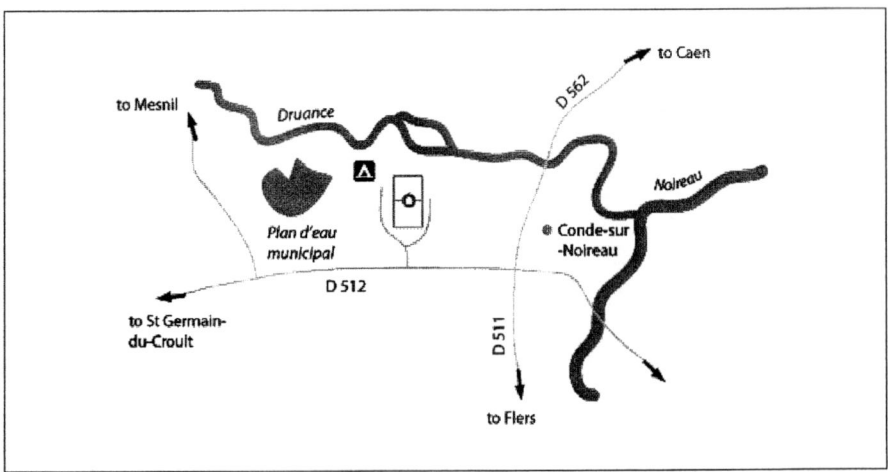

Day tickets and angling licences are available from: Graineterie Pêche, 1, rue Vaulegeard, 14110 Condé Sur Noireau Tel, 02 31 69 00 63. Café Bar, 9, place Colonel Candau, 14410 Vassy Tel, 02 31 68 51 63.

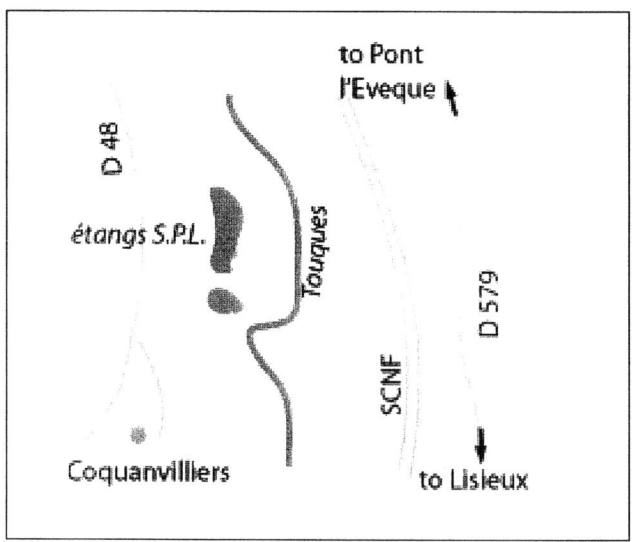

Sea Trout in Calvados

Calvados has fifteen rivers and streams that account annually for more than 1,500 sea trout caught up to 15cm long. The river Touques is one of the most famous rivers in France and it is thought to give up around 3,000 sea trout each season. And it is to this river on overcast June evenings that anglers are attracted.

September through October is also a good time to fish. Favourite fishing lures include rapalas, minnow imitations, spoons and imitation flies. Other sea trout rivers worth investigating include the lower Dives River, and between the confluence of the Laizon and the Vie is a stretch where an angler stands an excellent chance of bagging up.

On the river Orne the fish monitoring station has recorded an annual increase in fish numbers from 200 to 300 fish. Some specimens reach 3 kg. The sea trout season runs from May 14th through September 18th fishing for this species is only possible on water classified as sea trout. Refer to the départemental map. Fishing is permitted for up to two hours after sunset. When darkness falls the fish come alive.

Fly-fishing only is allowed for sea trout from 22nd September through 26th October on the river Touques between the RD 264 road bridge at Breuil-en-Auge and the département of Orne. On the river Dives downstream: of the D 40 road bridge at Saint Pierre sur Dives. River Orne downstream: from its confluence with river Maire at Sérans. River Seulles downstream: from the pont de Saint Gabriel. River Vire downstream from the RD 53 road bridge in Condé sur Vie – towns of Neuilly la Forêt and Isigny-sur-Mer.

On other waters fishing for sea trout is allowed from the second Saturday in May through 3rd Sunday in September. There is a 35cm minimum size limit.

The eel is caught everywhere. But especially so: in the river Orne and the marais côtiers - marshlands. Here you will still find anglers fishing with the ancient technique of vermée – a ball of worms on a cotton string requiring no hook. This technique works best in cloudy water with rain predicted. Large eel specimens are often taken using dead bait.

Zone E

The local angling club that manages this area is called La Guale Livarotaise, they can be contacted at: Mairie 14140 Livarot, 02 31 63 41 02 31 61 02 43.72/.

Places to fish: a 16 km stretch classified as private watercan be fished from the border with département de L'Orne until Coupesarte the fishing area is well signposted.

There is a 10-bag limit, 25cm minimum size. All restocking is carried out from theestate of M. Stauber – Planète Loisirs till just upstream of Boeufs Blancs. Fishing in the reserve is authorised from the right bank. The parcours mouche – fly-fishing stretch is situated downstream of the pont de Mesnil-Durand, it's well signposted.

Parcours de Pêche. River Vie upstream stretch.

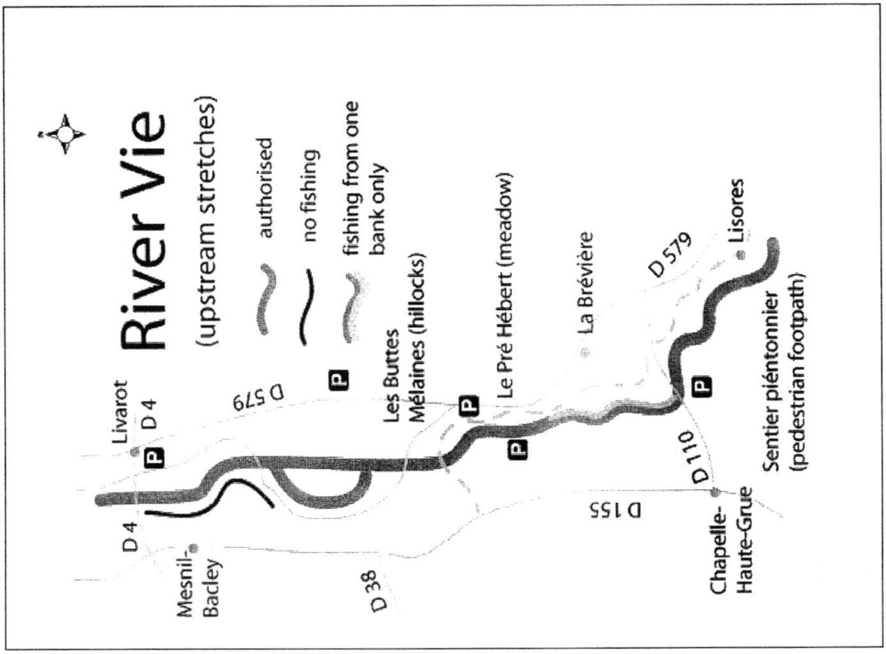

River Vie, downstream stretch

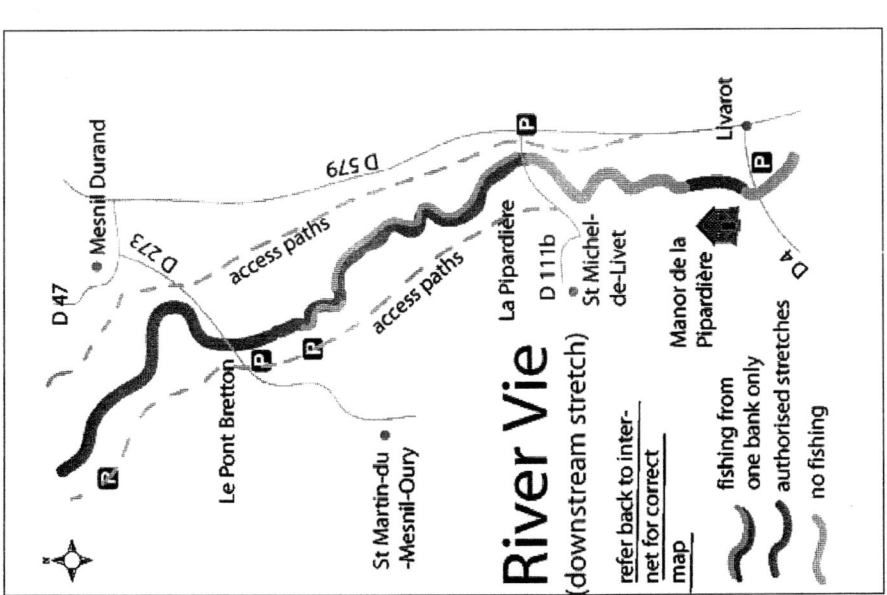

Licences and day tickets are available from.

Bar Le Galopin, 2, place Pasteur, 14140 Livarot Tel, 02 31 63 54 67. Office du Tourisme, 1, place Georges Bisson, 14140 Livarot Tel, 02 31 63 47 39.

The local angling club that manages this area is called La Guale Pétruvienne they can be contacted at: 52 route de Grisy, 14170 Saint Pierre Sur Dives Tel, 02 31 20 39 66/02 31 20 51 95.

Places to fish: river Dives from the pont de Vendeuvre to Ecajeul. Well signposted.

Fish present include trout, eels and poisson blanc - skimmers. Fishing is permitted on Saturday, Sunday, Wednesday and public holidays. And everyday after 13th May. No spinning is allowed till after 13th May. 8-bag limit, 25cm minimum size.

Recommended places to fish include by the Moulin d'Ouville and the site du Moulin de Carel.

Parcours de Pêche. River Dives: fishing stretch from Vendeuvre to Ecajeul.

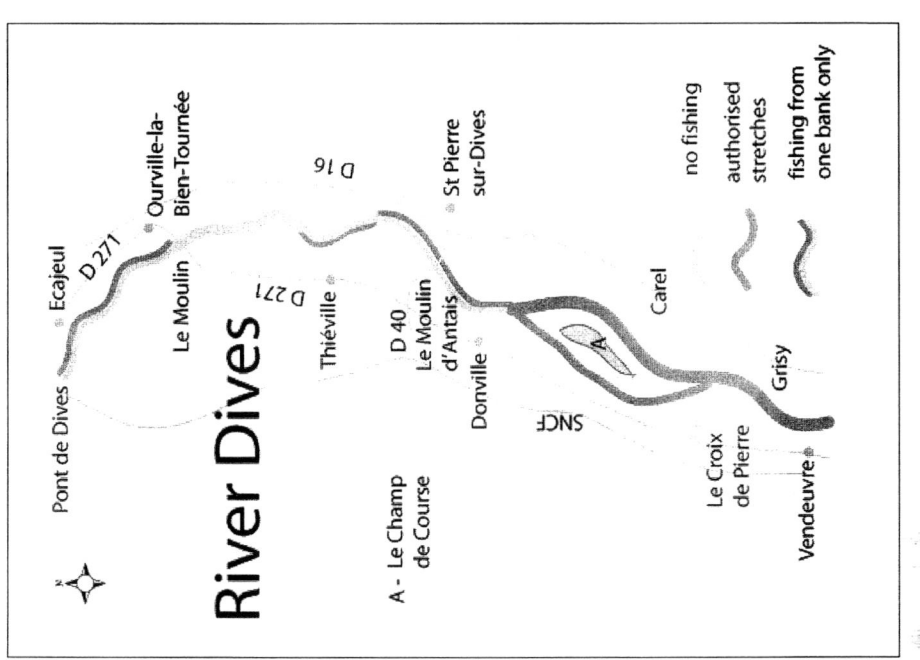

The local angling club that manages this area is called Le Laizon, they can be contacted at: Mairie 14420 Bons Tassilly, Tel, 02 31 40 77 43/06 15 94 22 49.

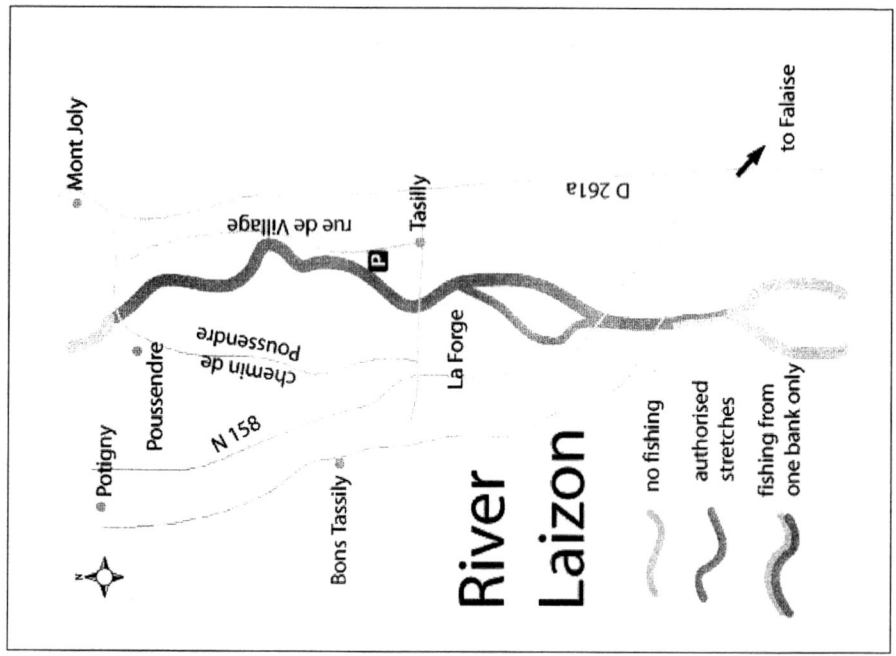

Places to fish: the River Laizon upstream and downstream of Bons-Tassilly. Fish caught by anglers include trout, eels and roach.

Parcours de Pêche. Fishing is possible from the Chemin de Poussendre - road to Pont Grimoult.

Zone F

The local angling club that manages this area is called Les Pêcheurs a la Ligne de la Vallée d'Auge, they can be contacted at: Mairie de Pont L'Evêque 14130 Pont L'evêque Tel, 0231640555 email: p.auzerais@mertz.fr or visit: www.apalva.new.fr

Places to fish

The river Touques is 109 km long it has the finest population of sea trout in France they can be caught downstream of Lisieux. But anglers can also catch trout and eels here. There are 80 km of bank to fish from these are divided into 19 parcours de pêche – fly-fishing only stretches including 9 parcours vocation touristique – tourist fishing stretches.

There is 25 km of bank to fish from the border downstream of the plan d'eau du Châonne near Breuil-en-Auge until just upstream of the domaine maritime by the pont SNCF de Touques.

The Haute Touques – upper valley begins for our purposes near Gacé after the confluence with the ruisseau de la Fontaine Bouillante. Channel width is 4-6m. It winds through a narrow valley whose steep slopes are known to locals as piquanes. There are shallow runs and riffs. The area is sparsely populated.

After the confluence with the ruisseau du Bourgel the channel widens to 6-12 m. And flows quickly towards the confluence with its main tributary the river Orbiquet situated at Lisieux.

Downstream from Lisieux begins the Basse Touques – lower valley. The channel broadens to 15-20 m. The gradient of the banks increases as it meanders through low-lying pasture. There are large pools and wide runs. The area is more densely populated.

The barrage de Breuil dam divides public from private fishing stretches. Visitors can fish both categories of water. But will require a local angling licence and a Timbre Migrateur pour la Truite de mer – additional sea trout fishing tax that is valid just for the river Touques. All the tributaries are classified as private water.

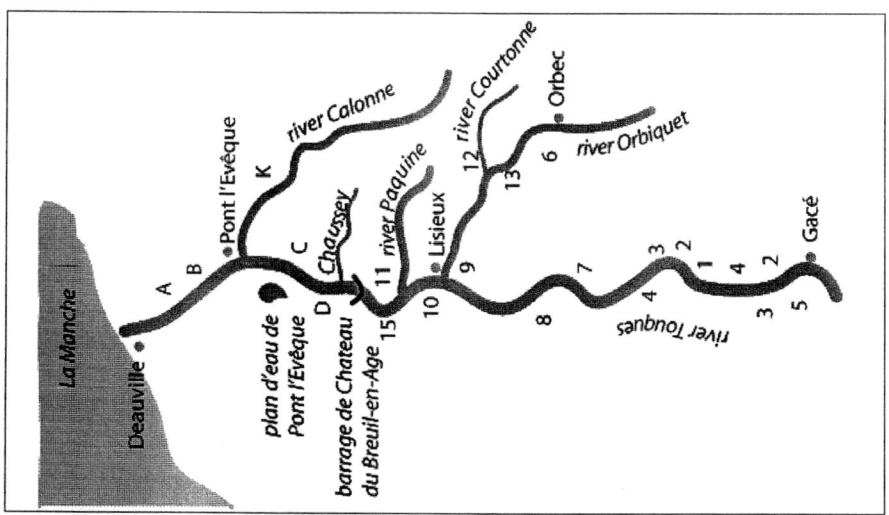

Detailed sketch maps are available for every parcours de pêche – fishing stretch listed below. Visit http://www.touques-parages.com/ now click on *parcours* then click on *impression plans* the maps are in pdf format

Parcours de pêche privee – private fishing stretches that everyone can fish

There are 6 parcours specifique - stretches covering 12 km of river: reserved for uniquely for fly-fishing that requires a mouche à la journée - fly-fishing day ticket in addition to your départemental annual angling licence or holiday angling licence to fish these private stretches.

On these river stretches anglers are encouraged to catch and release. Day tickets cost between €13 and €19. Annual licences specifically for these local stretches cost from: €121 to €138. Including fishing on the river Orne: €185 to €215. If you have this local fishing licence you will not require a day ticket or the Timbre migrateur – sea trout fishing tax.

Anglers will require the Timbre migrateur / taxe truite de mer – stamp in their angling licence in order to fish for sea trout on the river Touques. This is not required for the river Calonne where no sea trout are caught. It costs €33.5.

There are 7 parcours classique- traditional fishing stretches. Covering 18 km of river. Anglers can bag up in these areas. The annual licence costs €85, then €57 thereafter for renewal. Carte vacances costs €27.3 for a 15 consecutive day period: from 1st June through 18th September.

In total there are 15 parcours to choose from. May through August is a good time to visit. The fishing stretches are well signposted.

In general sedges and olive fly lures work well, size 4-5-line w/f, floating or intermediate, 8-9 foot rod. A rapid casting technique required on the upper stretches.

1. Vallee des Moutiers-Hubert situated between the D 46 and the Manoir de Cheffretau. Classified as a parcours mouche where only fly-fishing is allowed. 1.6 km stretch: fishing on both banks. Channel is between 5-10 m wide. Strong concentration of brown trout: between 20-30 cm. Some big'ns. Rainbow trout stopped being released on this stretch in

1999, but some specimens up to 40 cm are still caught. Wading is recommended when you can approach within 5 m of your quarry. The stretch is considered quite technical and requires short casts. The area around the manor is beautiful. The upstream reaches are wilder and the banks steeper. Recommended fly lure: La Thymallu, it works best in July and August. Request one from the local tackle shop.

2. Parc Hebert situated between Les Moutiers Hebert and Notre Dame de Courson. This stretch is classified as a parcours classique where any fishing technique is allowed. Fish along 1 km stretch from either bank. Select a black-sedge imitation fly lure in June and August. Tree lined banks through pasture capture a tranquil fishing experience.

3. Le Mirror de Courson situated between Notre dame de Courson and Moulin de Lyee. Fly-fishing only. You will require a trout fishing day ticket in addition to your regular licence. 935 m stretch on both banks. Favourite fly lure among local anglers is the small Araignée ailée in grey and red in June and July. Or small CDC. Trout here will exceed 50 cm.

4. Cascade situated between Moulin du Lyee and Fervaques. Fly-fishing only, a trout fishing day ticket required. 1 km stretch on both banks. Upstream of the waterfall fishing is good at dusk. Here the channel is between 5 and 8 m wide. On most of the upstream section the current is slow and there are deep pools. Rainbow trout are hard fighters and the brown trout has a varied livery.

Select a sedge CDC fly lure, size 12-18. Rod length 7 ½ – 8 ½ feet, size 4-5 line, floating or intermediate, fly lures to select include sedges and olives size 12-18. Anglers here also catch many good specimens using minnow and spinner lures weighing 8-20 grammes.

6. Moulin de Beauvoir, rivers Orbiquet and Orbec. All types of fishing allowed. 900 m stretch on both banks. A grey sedge fly lure is effective throughout the whole season. For sea trout use a rod between 9 ½ and 11 feet, size 7-8 intermediate line. For trout a 9-10 foot rod size 5-6 intermediate line.

The **river Orbiquet** in many ways is a typical chalk stream of the region that starts near Folletière-Abenon from underground caves that provide the river with a continual flow of clean water year round. A tributary the Courtonne contributes clean water.

7. L'Île de Prëtrevile situated between the pont d'Aucquainville and the pont de la Forge. Fly-fishing only. 5.16 km stretch along both banks. Orange nymph fly lures work well all season. 5-8 m wide, good choice of swims. Good access to the bank along its whole course. Lots of fish.

8. St Jean de Livet situated between La Forge and St Martin de la Lieue. Al methods allowed. 7.4 km stretch fishing along both banks. Select a Mouche de mai mi-foncé flt – dark mayfly fishing lure. Try short upstream casts at first, then, lengthen out.

9. Manoir St Hyppolyte situated between St Desir and St Martin de la Lieue. Fly-fishing only. 1.1 km stretch fish both banks. Emergent sedge fly lure recommended. Narrow channel fast and shallow, 7-10 m wide. The banks are high, making casting technical. The stretch is a series of mini-meanders. Lookout for deeper holes. Some sea trout present but mostly rainbow and brown trout.

10. Between Lisieux and river Paquine. All fishing methods are allowed. 3 km stretch on river Touques both banks. 1.7 km stretch of the river Paquine both banks. This is a more consistent fish than parcours numbers 11 and 15. Many deep pools encourage fishing for sea trout.

The **river Paquine** is a small river lasting 14 km but it enjoys peaceful surroundings near Lisieux. Lots of brown trout and sea trout are present.

11. Chateau de Bouttemont situated between river Paquine and Coquainvilliers. Fly-fishing only. 1660 m stretch on both banks. Downstream part, 15-28 m wide is best for fly-fishing especially for sea trout. Select a fly lure called the La Voiseux to attact them. From mid June through October. The bank is 1 m high. Be careful when wading because the depth can vary suddenly. Lovely brown trout are caught between 35-45 cm. There are some wonderful rainbow trout specimens also present.

12. Glos, river Orbiquet. All fishing methods are allowed. 625 m stretch right bank only. Golden headed nymph works well here.

13. Saint Pierre de Maill OC, river Orbiquet. All methods allowed. 1.4km stretch both banks. Recommended fly is La Peute for year round use. Mostly straight channel, moderate flow, little cover. Clear water makes the fish wary. Go light on tackle. Brown trout are present.

15. Between the Chateau de Bouttemont and le Breuil-en-Auge. All fishing methods allowed. 3 km stretch on both banks. Between 15-18 m wide. From May through June select a mouche de mai Claire fly lure. On this stretch together with parcours number 11 is the best sea trout fishing on the private stretches. Specimen brown and rainbow trout are also present. Take care when wading because the channel bed is uneven.

Parcours de Pêche - fishing stretches

River Touques: from Fierville-les-Parcs to Touques.

A. Parcours de pêche public – fishing stretch classified as public water, in totality from downstream of the plan d'eau du Château du Breuil en Age, on the river Touques from the pont du chemin-de-fer (railway: Lisieux-Deauville) to 250 m from the Pont de Touques.

Situated upstream of the domaine maritime - estuary, from the pont SCNF du Touques – railway bridge to the pont de la D 58 road bridge connecting St Martin with Chartrans. Recommended fly lure is La Tissié's. This stretch is tidal. The river course follows a series of regular, broad, slow and deep meanders. The more interesting reach is upstream of the GDF railway line in particular towards the pont de Roncheville. Lighten up on your tackle when fishing on the ebb tide. This stretch rewards spinning. But fly-fishermen can still bag up using a large wet fly lure.

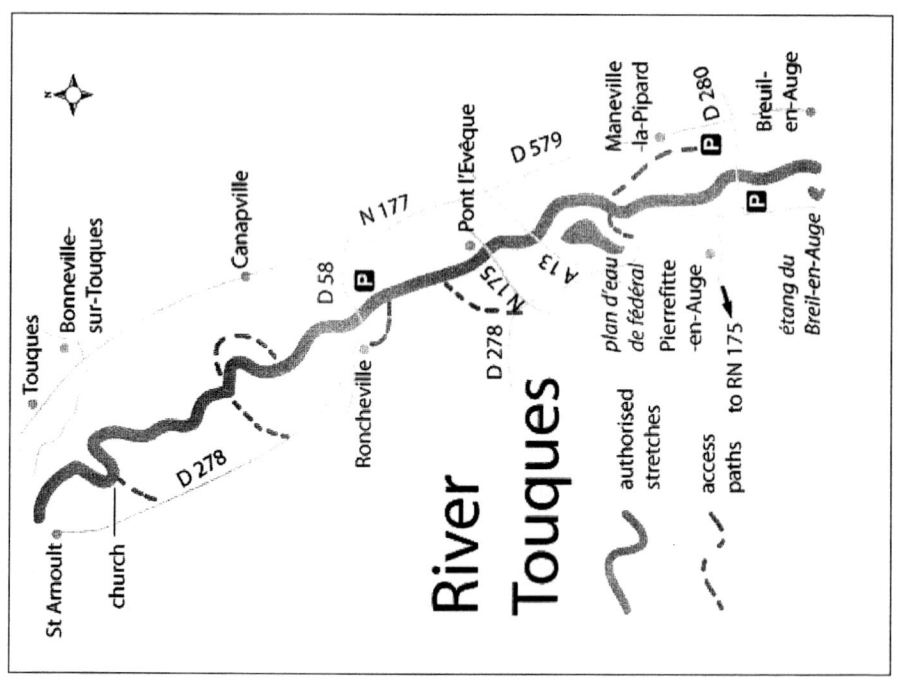

An 11-13 foot fly rod is recommended using 7-8 size line. Lures include minnows, spinners, spoons and wobblers.

B. Downstream of Pont L'Eveque fish from the pont de la D 58 road bridge at Roncheville to the pont de la N 175 road bridge at Pont L'Eveque. Le Renard fly lure is a good choice for this stretch.

This is a varied stretch with interesting flow characteristics. Open bank upstream, downstream banks bordered by trees. In short a very good place to fly-fish for sea trout. Upstream of the rapids the sea trout are caught under the trees along the right bank. Towards dusk the fish swim out into the current so then cast a fly to the left bank.

C. From pont de la N 175 upstream of Pont L'Eveque to the pont de la D280A at Pierrefitte en Aug. Fly lure to use is the Green Butt. This stretch contains a mixture of sea trout and brown trout. Just upstream of Pont L'Eveque there is a series of meanders are perfect for fly and near the Pont de Pierrefitte where the channel is shaded by alders spinning is king.

D. Upstream border of the water classified as domaine public: situated from the pont de la D 280A at Pierrefitte en Auge to the Chateau de Breuil en Auge. Select La Perruche fly lure. This stretch has two characteristics. The upstream reach is deep and slow and the downstream reach beginning by the cornfield has many runs where spinning bags the larger fish. Wet fly-fishing techniques succeed by the cornfield. Cast beyond the middle current then retrieve your fly lure with a series of small tugs. On sunny days the fish hold up by the bank. When overcast and at dusk the fish will occupy the main channel.

K. River Calonne, three stretches. Select a Fourmi fly lure. The water is classified as domaine privé. The parcours du moulin de Quincampoix contains slow and deep swims especially upstream of the D 162. Here there are lots of alder trees bank side, ultra-léger is the technique that works best here. There are two more stretches to fish further upstream. The furthest, above the D 534 is the most interesting. Here a series of runs and pools supports a good head of trout. A fly lure comes in handy especially at dusk. These stretches are explained in more detail below.

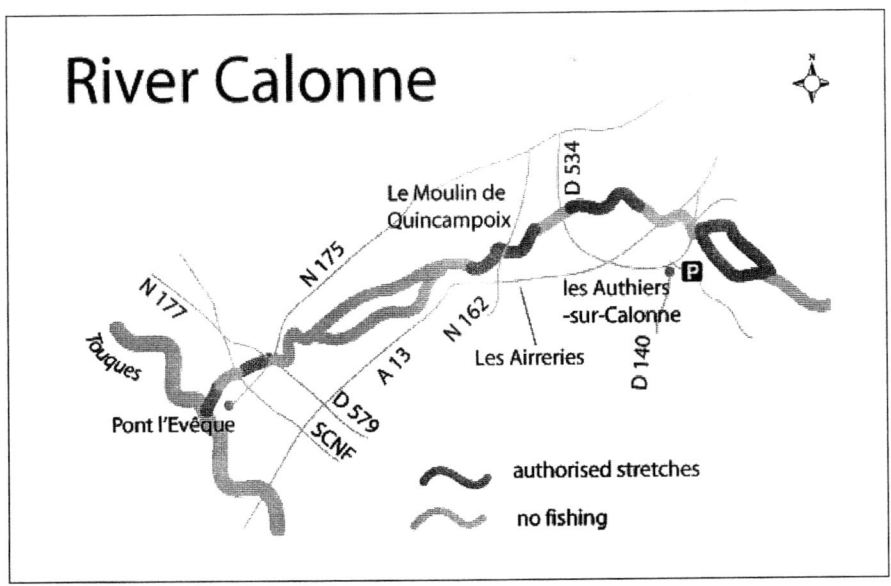

River Calonne: from Fierville-les-Parcs to Touques.

The **river Calonne** and main tributary is one of the most beautiful of the Basse Touques – lower valley where anglers catch, brown trout and eel.

It is favourable to fish reproduction especially sea trout because it is the first significant tributary on the journey to fish spawning grounds. But only rarely are sea trout caught herebecause the channel is too narrow. The sea trout hold up deep under the bank and venture forth after nightfall.

The banks are accessible and well maintained by the local angling club. There are 6 parcours de pêche, all well signposted. These contain lots of fishing platforms and deeper pools. There is one parcours de pêche reserved for junior anglers under 16 years of age. Parcours privé – private fishing reserves require the angler to be in pocession of the Carte de pêche APALVA – Calvados angling licence, there is no reciprocity with other départements for these particular waters. But these private fishing reserves are open to anglers from other départements. Trout are stocked in March, April, may. June and September. No fishing is allowed at weekends after stockings. Check with the angling federation for details: Email: peche.calvados@wanadoo.fr

Parcours de pêche K1 under 16's only: fish to the Pont l'Evêque, from the pont de la RN 177 until 100 m after the pont SNCF Chaussée Nival on both two banks up to the confluence with the bras de Mars at Touques. Spinning is not permitted until 14th June.

Parcours de pêche K2 Bras de Mars: from the confluence of Bras de Mars until the river Touques.

Parcours de pêche K3 les Authieux sur Calonne (autoroute): on both banks from the first pont de la D 534 until the pont de l'A 13 (1.8 km stretch).

Parcours de pêche K4 St Julien sur Calonne: take the RN 175 from the D 162 heading for St Julien sur Calonne, on both banks from every bridge point.

Parcours de pêche K5 les Authieux sur Calonne (bourg): take the D 534, 1.5 km stretch to Authieux sur Calonne.

Parcours de pêche K6 la Thironnière: take the D 534, access between Authieux sur Calonne and Bonneville la Louvet on the left. Fishing only from the right bank. In order to preserve the natural habitat – flora and fauna this reserve is not stocked

Minimum caught fish size is 30cm in order to preserve a mature breeding population of brown trout. 6-bag limit for a mixture of brown and rainbow trout. 6-bag limit for sea trout, 35cm minimum size. Spinning is not allowed until after the opening of the sea trout season.

Volunteers for working parties, to clean riverbanks are welcome on the third Saturday in each month except July and August. The meeting point is at the place du Marché at the Pont l'Evêque. Tel, 0231640555: for details.

L'étang du Breuil-en-Auge (2.5 ha) 1st category. Thw whole family will enjoy fishing here. Fish species present include rainbow trout, pike, zander, roach, carp, eels and a good many other species. Day tickets are available anglers are not required to purchase the more expensive angling départemental licences. For trout fishing additional payment is required when you purchase your day ticket. Trout are stocked from May to October. For details Tel, 0231640555 or 0686677551.

L'étang du Breuil-en-Auge: situated next to the turn-off from Beruil-en-Auge on the D 579, between Lisieux and Pont l'Evêque.

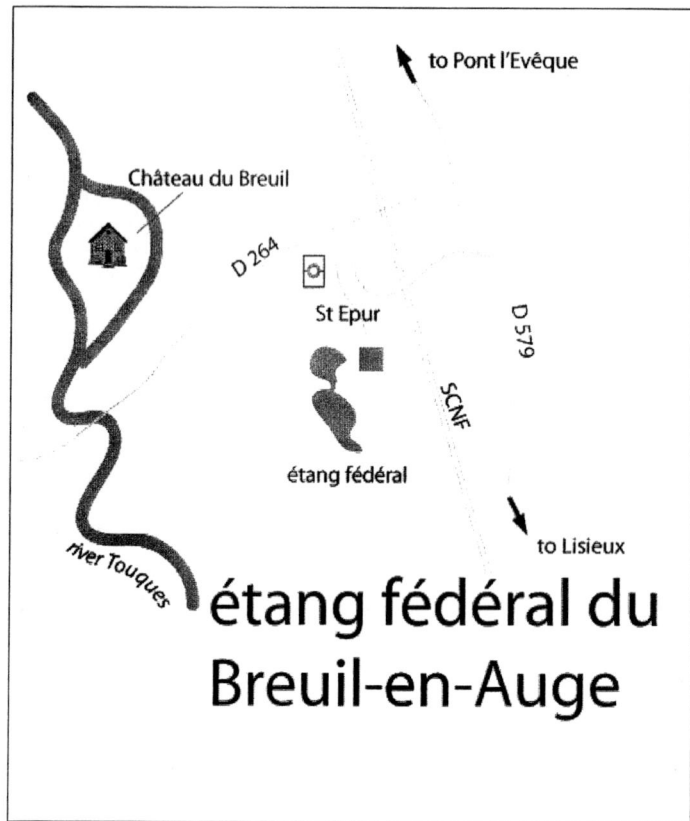

Except for pike and zander – the trout season runs from the 2nd Saturday in May through 31st January the lake is open for anglers all year. There is a 6-bag limit for trout. 3-rod limit.

Methods permitted are natural baits, fly-fishing, ledgering, float fishing and fishing a bubble float with fly droppers.

Day tickets and licences for this lake are available from: Bar tabac restaurant Le Relais du Breuil - Le Bourg - Le Breuil-en-Auge. Pascal La Planche - Articles de Pêche - Place du Calvaire - Pont l'Evêque. Décathlon - la Folletière – Lisieux.

Prices for day tickets and annual season ticket for the lake

Affiliated to APALVA and AAPPMA du Calvados – those anglers who have an angling licence purchased in Calvados département.
Carte adulte: Journalière: €10; annuelle: €50; vacances (1): €30
Carte jeune: Journalière: €5 ; annuelle: €25; vacances (1): €15

Affiliated to AAPPMA de France - those anglers who have an angling licence purchased outside Calvados.

Carte adulte: Journalière: €14; annuelle: €60; vacances (1): €30
Carte jeune: Journalière: €7; annuelle: €30; vacances (1): €15

Those anglers who are not in pocession of any angling licence
Carte adulte: Journalière: €16; annuelle: €95; vacances (1): €30
Carte jeune: Journalière: €8; annuelle: €47.50; vacances (1): €15

Local angling club called Touques-Parages can be contacted at: 14 rue de Verdun, 14100 Lisieux. Tel, 0231313742 fax: 02.31.62.54.95 Email: parages @wanadoo.fr

Parcours de pêche, fishing stretches located in the département de l'Orne

1. Coulmer, from Orgeras To Gacé. All methods of angling allowed. Anglers must be in pocession of the Carte de Pêche. 2.7 km stretch fishing from both banks. Recommended fly lure is Araignée ailée grise jaune – daddy long legs in grey and yellow.

2. Mardilly, from Mardilly to Neuville sur Touques. 4.8 km stretch both banks. All fishing methods allowed. Except for the upstream parts: that are reserved for fly-fishing only and is catch and release. The Pheasant tail is the choice of fly lure along this stretch. Anglers must be in pocession of the Carte de Pêche.

3. Le Gabion, from Neuville sur Touques to the embouchure du Chamont – water inlet. All fishing methods allowed. Anglers must be in pocession of the Carte de Pêche. 1.9 km stretch both banks. At this point the river Touques is 5-7 m wide. It meanders across the pastures. Depth varies greatly. The channel bed is made up of gravel, sand and stones depending on site. Fly lure of choice is the CDC Lièvre – hare's ear.

4. Le Pigeonnier, from the D 33 to Manoir de Ticheville. Parcours a mouche – fly-fishing only stretch. Anglers will require a carte spécifique mouche"à la journée – trout fishing day ticket in addition to a Carte de Pêche. 6.2 km stretch both banks. 7-8 m wide. Depth varies from 30 cm to 3 m. Fly lure of choice is the cream sedge. Deep pools

interlink shallow faster runs. There are calm stretches followed by cascades. Rainbow trout are stocked but the wild brown trout are left to their owm devices. There are mostly wild brown trout and grayling rangig from 35-45cm present.

5. Stevroult de Montfort, from St Leonard to Gace. Fly-fishing only. Additional trout day ticket required. 1.5 km long both banks. Fly lure to use is the demi-palmer size 18-20. At this point the narrow channel is very enclosed. Wild brown trout predominate. Use light tackle.

6. Le Paradis, from Pontchardon to Canapville. Fly-fishing only. Additional trout day ticket required. 3.7 km stretch both banks. Interesting stretch alternating between woods and fields. Choice of fly lure is Le sedge roux – ginger. Good head of trout downstream of the confluence with the ruisseau de Bourgel. Some specimen grayling are present. The bank is narrower than on parcours number 4 and more trees are present. From the ruisseau de Bourgel there are calmer runs. Brown trout reach 35-40cm.

A fish ladder has been created on the Orne section of the river Tourques at the Moulin de la Scierie at Notre Dam de Coursen. This opens up one third of the total river basin to spawning brown trout.

Sea trout

Commonly known in France as Truite Saumonée or Truite Argentée.

Their season starts on second Saturday in May and ends on the last Sunday in October. Fishing is allowed until two hours after sunset except on the river Calonne. From 19th September until 30th October only fly-fishing is allowed. 35cm minimum size, 6-bag limit iand t is appreciated if anglers report their catches. The largest recorded sea trout recorded in 2005 by the fish counter at barrage de Breuil measured 79cm. 32 salmon were also counted.

The sea trout always prefers calmer water to conserve energy. On downstream stretches of the river Touques fish activity will coincide with the rising tide at dusk. Sea trout do not venture past Lisieux.

The sea troutrun up the river Toques begins around 20th May when the temperature of the river rises above 15c. The biggest fish arrive early followed by younger fish in much larger number by mid July. After a gap period there is a final rush of fish in October. Spawning takes place in the second half of December. Only the smaller sea trout feed in freshwater. Sea trout have brown orange spots on their fins while brown trout in the river Touques have red points on their fins.

Up to 20 fish ladders were installed to increase their numbers. In 1998 sea trout stocks were estimated between 3000-4000: according to the monitoring station on the river Calonne. In 2002 the figure had increased to 5000-6000 fish. But this figure only represent those fish counted in the final third of the river downstream.

40% of catches are carried out in the last 6 weeks of the fishing season. Half of captures come after dusk. Most are caught using fly lures between Lisieux and the Pont de Rocheville. A rod measuring 10 ½ -13 feet, line number 6-8, the longer rod will enable the angler to cast over the long grass while remaining hidden at the foot of the bank. Especially the stretch: downstream of Pont l'Evêque.

A dry fly will usually attract smaller fish. To catch the larger specimens select a wet fly use an intermediate line or a floating line with a sinking leader. Select small streamer fly lures – these imitate fish fry. Larger streamer fly lures prove more effective after dusk.

Traditional fly lures to use on the Touquet include the La Perruche – budgie feather and La Voiseux. Essentially any fly lure that you select should not be over dressed. Semi-rigged hair from a fox or stoat is appropriate. The Hairy Mary or La Tréportaise work well.

Dark colours, black, chestnut and purple with a touch of silver prove attractive to fish. Finished of with a hint of red or orange. Double hooks can ad ballast when fishing light. If there is a lot of visible activity on the water at dusk select a dry fly lure for the takes.

Cast downstream at a 75 degree angle, laying-off line with the current drift to the far bank. Then employ a soft retrieve, use no sharp movement. Mornings and overcast days are good times to fish in addition to most evenings.

Spinning works best during the day because the lure can access deep bank recesses that the fly lure cannot. Especially: upstream of Pont l'Evêque. Minnow lures are a favourite with anglers fishing here. At dusk Rapala spinners work well: in silver, blue or orange 6-8cm. Spoons work best after rain in autumn.

Sea trout migrate up other rivers in Normandy and Brittany but the river Touques is the prettiest. Sea trout also migrate up the river basins of the Adour, Garonne, Charente, Loire and Rhine.

Brown trout

Commonly know in France as Mouchetée, Troucia, Trouette, Truche, Truiton and Zébrée.

Downstream of Lisieux: the minimum caught size is 25cm, 8-bag limit. Upstream of Lisieux, minimum size is 30cm, 5-bag limit. Season runs from 2nd Saturday in March through 3rd Sunday in September.

Upstream of Lisieux and on the river Orne: season runs from 12th March through 18th September. Here the channel is narrower and shallower. Trout hold up under branches and tree stumps. In spring they move out into the runs and pools.

Fishing is good from Lisieux to Notre Dam. Select a 7 ½ – 8 ½ foot rod, line size 4-5. Fish with dry flies in spring cast to the bank. Select baetidés – olives imitation fly lures or sedges. In May select mayflies that work very well at dusk. Mornings are just as good.

July and August present a greater challenge for the dry fly exponent. Small ephemeras and dipteros make up most of the hatchings. Reduce hook size to 16 and select small emerger fly imitations CDC. September brings hatchings of tricopteros and winged ants.

During the day use a wet fly, sedges can prove effective but the upstream stretches of the Touques do not encourage fishing by sight. Use an intermediate line. Streamers are effective in faster currents in spring.

The channel broadens out downstream of Lisieux. Nice specimen trout are located on downstream stretches of the Touques from Lisieux as far as Roncheville. But the very best fishing is between Lisieux and Pont L'Evêque. For dry fly fishing the rod needs to be 9-9 ½ feet, size 5 line, w/f for longer casts. Best periods to fish are from April through mid June then again from end of August through middle of September.

During the day the trout stay close to the bank. At this time: use wet fly lure tactics. Select an emergent mayfly imitation nfly lure at the start of the season then use tricoptero imitation fly lures a little later on. At dusk the trout come into the current looking for flies on the surface, select dry fly lures at this time of the day.

Dry flies at dusk. In spring select baetides and ephemera imitation fly lures. In July select tricopteros imitations. From mid August through September: select ant imitations. A black gnat imitation is a safe bet to use throughout the season.

For wet fly fishing, during the day use a rod between 10-11 feet, size 4-5 line, don't fish too fine and avoid fast action rods which will not be able to absorb the shock of heavy bites. There are plenty of larvae in the water so the choice of wet fly lures is wide. Tricopteros imitations are very effective.

Grayling are just starting to be introduced into this river basin. There is a catch and release policy for this fish species.

Angling licences for this area are available from:

Auberge de la Vallee, L'Eglise, Coquanvilliers Tel, 0231622920

Decathlon, La Folletière, Lisieux Tel, 0231486040

Tourisme de Lisieux - cartes vacances and cartes mouche – trout fishing day tickets only, on sale from 1st june to 30th September.
11 rue d'Alençon, 14106 Lisieux Cedex
Tel, 0231481810 fax, 0231481811
Email: tourisme@cclisieuxpaysdauge.fr

The Liseuix Tourisme offers 2 night bed and breakfast stays including two days fishing the river Touques including licence for €125.

Mondial Pêche, rue Marcelin Berthelot, Mondeville Tel, 0231830020

La Planche, 1 bis rue Georges Clemenceau, 14130 Pont Levéque 0231640077

La Planche 1bis rue Georges Clemenceau, Pont Léveque Tel, 0231640077

Tourisme, Pont Léveque Tel, 0231641277

Bar-tabac 'La bonne franquette' Le Breuil en Auge Tel, 0231.650794

Le Restaurant du Tourisme, 19 place du Général de Gaulle, Cormeilles, Eure Tel, 0232578007

Angling licences for Orne Département are available from:

M. Launstorfer, Moulin du Lyée, Notre Dam de Courson: open from 9am to noon and 2pm to 7pm www.launstorfer.com Tel, 0231322725 Email: info@launstorfer.com

Tourisme de Gacé, Place du Château, Gacé, open from 01/07 to 31/08 Tel, 0233355024

The angling association responsible for the management of the Touques river basin in its entirety can be contacted at:

K. Emmanuel Therin, 14 rue de Verdun, 14100 Lisieux France
Tel, 0231313742, fax, 02.31625495, from U.K. Tel, 0(33) 231313742, fax, 0 (33) 231625495 Email: parages@wanadoo.fr

Societé Pêche Lisieux. F. Faucher, 2 rue Robida, 14100 Lisieux Tel, 0231329132. This angling club manages the private stretches upstream of Breuil en Age on the rivers Touques, Orbiquet and Paquine.

L'Association des Pêcheurs à la ligne de la vallée d'Auge A.P.A.L.V.A. are based at Pont Léveque and manages the Touques river basin downstream of the barrage de Breuil en Age. Contact: Philippe Auzerais Tel, 0610967569

Guides de Pêche - fishing guides. I strongly recommend that you ask after one of these experts if you are a first timer to the area. Skills picked up in one day will save you time and energy for the rest of your trip.

Jean-Marc LeDot specialises in sea trout.
30 rue de l'Eglise, 14250 Port-en-Bessin
Tel, 0231214853
Mobile 0613628973
www.espritpeche.com
Email: espritpeche@cegetel.net

Thierry Wieser
Mobile 0617494390
www.pechesportive95.com
Email: pechesportive95@club-internet.fr

Jean Claude Delange 7, Avenue du Genéral-Leclerc, 14700 Falaise Tel, 0231407030, mobile 0673548414, Jean specialises in catching sea trout on the lower Touques.

MORBIHAN (56)

For more information contact: Fédération du Morbihan pour la Pêche et la Protection du Milieu Aquatique
3 rue Marcel Dassault - BP 10079 - 56892
Saint-Ave Cedex
Tel, 02 97 44 54 55 - Fax. 02 97 44 54 60
E-mail: fedepeche56@wanadoo.fr

Angling licence costs €1 for under 10's. Under 16's 14 or 24 including trout and salmon fishing, Carte Complète – €68.50: plus €33.50 EHGO if you want to fish in other départements. To fish for salmon an additional tax of €33.50 is payable. Carte Vacances, fishing for 15 consecutive days valid from 1st June through 17th September – €30 for coarse angling: 48 for trout and salmon fishing.

Trout season from 11th March through 17th September. 20cm minimum size, 10-bag limit, 23cm on salmon rivers. Minimum size for salmon is 50cm. Bag limit is three salmon. Wading is allowed. Contact the départemental angling federation mentioned above for details.

River Blavet – Martial Le Dortz an expert fly-angler offers his thoughts on a highly rated Bretagne river.

"Considered to be one of the most beautiful rivers in Brittany. Up to 2000 salmon were netted annually at Lochrist by the mouth of the river Blavet towards the end of the 19th century. At that time anglers, many were British caught 90% of their catches by écluses – locks on the lower reaches between Gorrets and Quellennec.

Since then the construction of new fish ladders have opened up the higher reaches. Salmon now spawn in the Saar, Hoed, Evel and Tarun affluents. Anglers followed suite and the 15 locks from Polvern to Boterneau give up good salmon on a regular bisis. In 2002 the ban was lifted on fishing within 50 m downstream of locks, encouragement for anglers fishing the upper reaches.

The best time for fishing: in summer and at end of the season are at the end of these run-offs from the locks. However often au toc anglers –

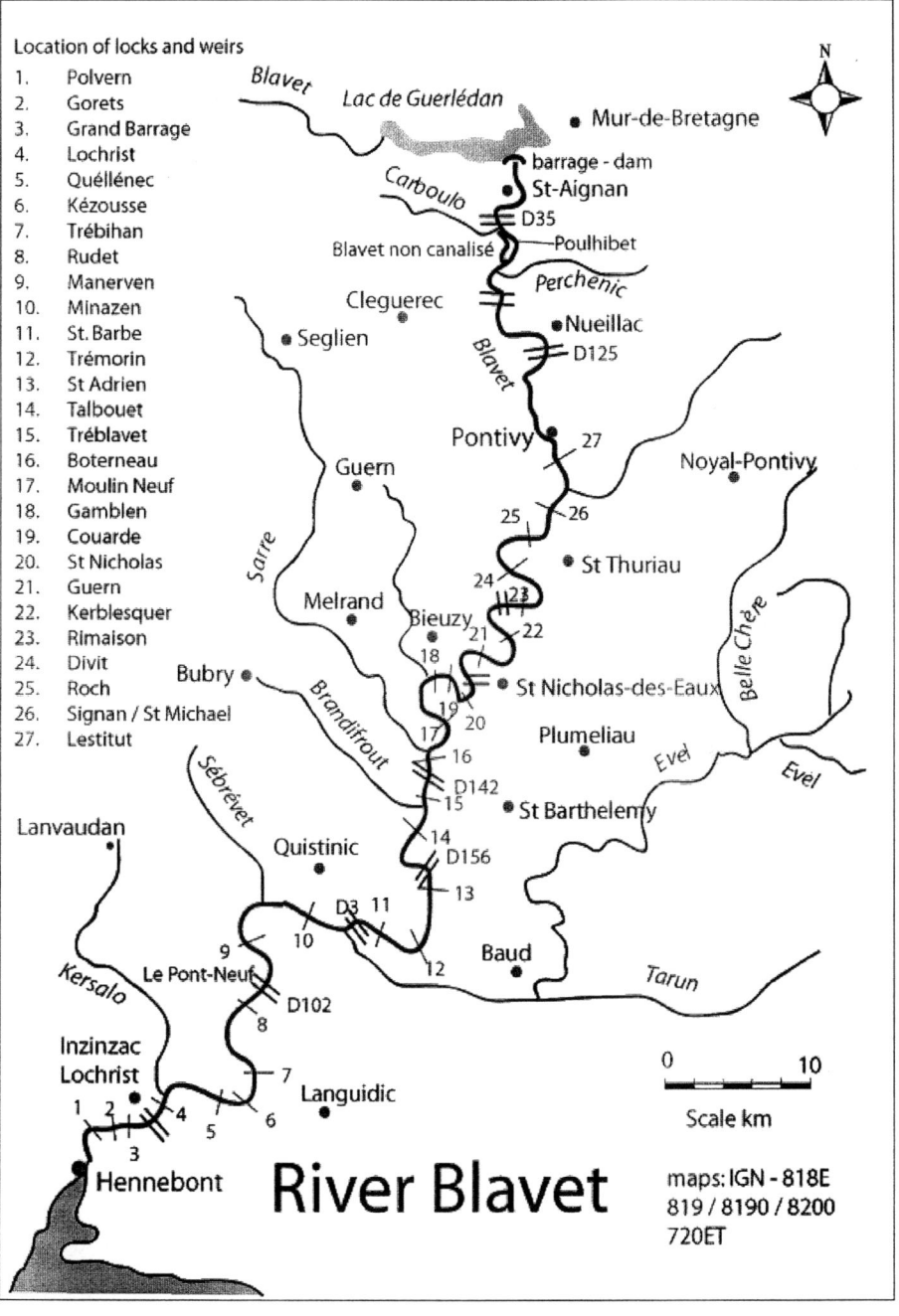

those who fish with bait such as shrimp can monopolise these positions and take these swims early.

Another problem for fly-fishermen is low water in summer, water management at HEP dams can affect flow. Local anglers will travel by car to fish several locks in one day. Visitors are advised to purchase IGN maps because access roads and tracks to these locks can prove tricky.

The locks at Quellennec, Trébihan, Manerwen and Budet are very pleasant places to fish. The barrages de Manerwen and Minazen are also good. At Minazen tree lined-banks give advantage to the wader. Gorrets is also worth a visit.

Local anglers use a two-handed 14-foot rod in order to cover the far bank. All salmon fly lures work well in Brittany. Favourite lures include wings made from poil d'écureuil or martre – squirrel or martin hair that vibrate in the outflow channel of locks. E.g. double hook Kamasan B280 N° 8.

Hackle: red cockerel feather. Tag: small red silkworm. Body: dubbing SLF black. Rib: tinsel round silver plated on half of the body, the side eyelet, on other half, a black hackle rolled up in a spiral; the wing consists of a pinch of squirrel hair in yellow tints surmounted by another pinch dyed in black.

This favourite fly pattern landed the author four salmon in the first half of October at the écluse de St Adrien. Sea trout and mullet are also caught on the river Blavet in summer and shad are a speciality by the barrage des Gorrets.

It's not all god news. In 1991-1992, the nitrate flow in the Evel river basin - a tributary of the Blavet River was 20,000 tons. In 2003 it was 60,000 tons."

There is a parcours de pêche - catch and release fly-fishing only stretch for trout starting from the barrage de St Aignan downstream to the Pont de Corboulo. Average channel width is 20 m average depth is 1 m. There are some large trout here. Angling licences and day tickets are available in Pontivy from the Magasin Ardent Pêche - shop. Map IGN 818Est – east.

Anglers can fish for salmon on the river Blavet downstream from the pont de chemin de fer – railwaybridge, situated at Pontivy. A tributary the river Sarre: downstream from the pont du CD 142 de Baud at Guémené sur Scorff known as Pont Sarre, at Guern.

Fish for trout on the river Kersalo, from the Étang du Ty Mad downstream to the Pont Yvon, 3 m wide, 0.5 m deep. Map IGN 820 Ouest, angling licence available from Bar PMU in Lochrist.

Nearby river with salmon stretches include: river Ellé situated just west of the river Blavet. In particular at the Loge Coucu, 1.7 km downstream of the bridge, rive Meslan. Map – IGN 719. Angling licences are available from: Bar Chez Gene, Lanvégen.

Salmon fishing is also possible on the river Scorff. Average channel width is 25 m, depth from 1-2 m. Fish from: the Moulin de Saint-Yves downstream to the Moulin de Princes. Fishing at the second ouverture – opening is recommended. Angling licences are available from Bar Le Bistrot, at bas Pont Scorff. Map – IGN 720 Est.

There is also good trout fishing on the river Scorff from the Pont Moulin à papier downstream to the village of Fanquigo. And from: Poulhibet downstream to the Moulin du Stang. Angling licences are available from Bar Tabac PMU and Café des Sportifs in Plouay. Map – IGN 720 and 719 Est. Anglers may also fish for salmon on the following stretches only.

River Naïc: downstream from the pont du CD 177 - road bridge.

River Inam or Steir-Laër: downstream from the pont du CD de Scaer to Gourin at place known as Kerbiquet at Gourin. Angling licences are available from: Magasin Chasse Pêche in Gourin. There is good trout fishing on this river from the Pont de Lutins downstream to the Pont de Rosmellec. Map – IGN 618 Est.

Ruisseau du Moulin du Duc: downstream from the Pont du Duc (ex RN 169) near the Moulin du Duc at Saint and Langonnet. Good trout fishing from the Moulin de Kertanguy downstream to the Moulin du Duc, 1.5m wide, 0.7m deep. Map – IGN 718 Est, angling licences are available from Magasin Chasse Pêche in Gourin.

Ruisseau de Pont Rouge or Aër: downstream from the Pont de Borne between Crosity and saint Tugdual.

River Brandifout or Ruisseau de la Croix Rouge: downstream from the pont du CD 3 de Bruby to Baud, at Bubry.

River Evel dowsntream: from the pont du CD 779 de Vannes to Baud to Brandivy.

River Tarun: downstream from the confluence with the ruisseau de Kerguillaue – left bank, at Locminé.

Trout fishing is available on the following river stretches

Vannes area: river Liziec, from Lescouedec downstream mto Tréalvé. This is a fast stretch 2.8 m wide and 0.8 m deep. Angling licences are available from Bar Le Vincebnnes in St Avé. Map- IGN 921 Est.

Vannes area: River Arz, from Moulin de Luhan downstream to the Pont de Guel. 4-5m wide, 1m deep. Angling licences are available from Bat-Tabac L'Escale in Monterblanc.

Gorin area: ruisseau Le Moulin du Pré. Fish from the Pont du Moulin Pré downstream to the Moulin de Kerbiquet. 2 m wide, 0.6 m deep. Map IGN 618 Est. Angling licences are available from Magasin Chasse Pêche in Gourin.

Gorin area: river Aër fish from the Pont er Born downstream to the Pont Ruoge. 4-5 m wide and half a metre deep. Some fast runs. Map IGN 718 Est, angling licences are available from Bar Le Triskell in Croisty.

Scorff valley area: river Kergustan from Bourg de Lignol downstream to the Moulin de Kerlautre, 3 m wide, 0.5 m deep. The stretch contains a succession of long wide runs. Map IGN 719 Est. Angling licence available from Café-Snack in Lignol.

River Scorff: fish from the Pont de Bot-Bihan downstream to the Moulin de Tronscorff, 3 m wide, 0.6 m deep. Map Ign 818 Est. Angling licence available from bar L'Odyssée in Guémené.

River Scorff: fish from the Pont du Stum downstream to the Pont de Brodimon, 10-12 m wide, 1.2 m deep. Slow stretch with deep holes. Map IGN 719 Est. Angling licence available from Restaurant and Bar Tabac in Inguiniel.

ILLE-ET-VILAINE (35)

In the département of Ille-et-Villaine there are 5,000 km of water to fish including over 1,000km of 1st category fishing and many lakes stocked with trout. The area is managed in cooperation with 27 local angling clubs.

Fishing on the on the river Vilaine is especially good for large zander. In addition salmon are caught on the river Couesnon and the numbers caught keep increasing. Around the area of Redon American largemouth Black bass predominate. They are a great fish to catch with streamers or popper fly lures using light tackle.

For more information contact:	Fédération de l'Ille-et-Vilaine pour la Pêche et la Protection du Milieu Aquatique, 9 rue Louis Kérautret Botmel - CS 26713 - 35067 Rennes Cedex Tel. 0299228180 - Fax 02 99 22 81 81 E-mail: federation.de.peche.35@wanadoo.fr

The river Couesnon is located in north east of the département Ille-et-Vilaine. It offers considerable possibilities for the fly angler. It is 100 km long, covering 1000 km sq of water; the whole river basin has 1000 km of rivers and streams.

In the 1980's this river experienced up to 25 cases of reported pollution annually. Since then salmon have been successfully reintroduced. It's a mixed bag for trout. They have been a success on the river Loysance and its tributaries, but on the main river Couesnon although water quality is good the trout population is at present unsustainable – large numbers are stocked, even though bigger fish are caught there is are enough juveniles present to sustain a viable population. There are 25-30 salmon per 100 m sq compared to only 5 trout. Compared with 73 trout per 100m sq on the Loysance River: where one of its affluents produces ten times as many

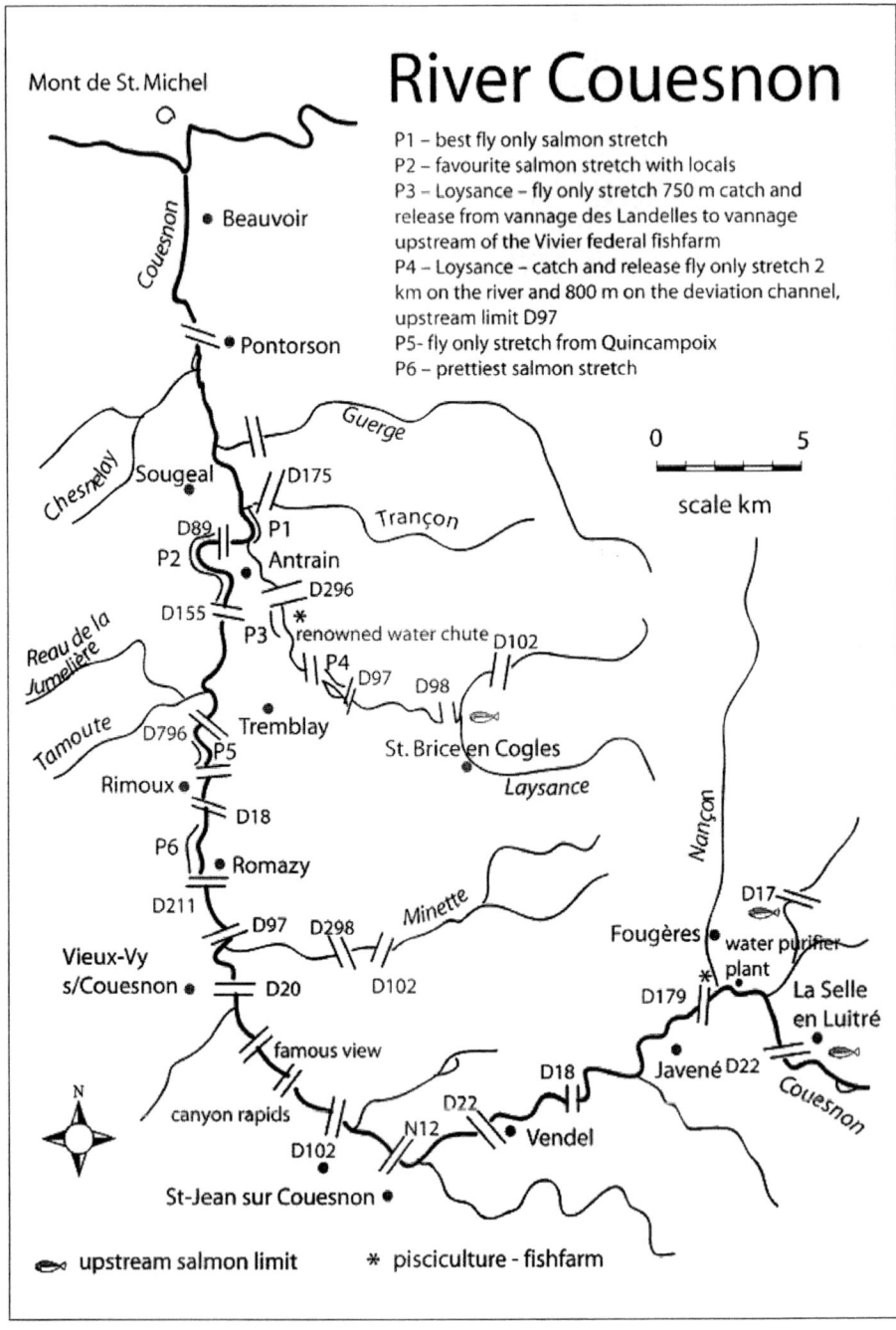

juvenile trout. Even though all trout fry for both rivers were sourced from the same fish farm.

The Couesnon has a current too strong for young fish to thrive, although salmon and sea trout prefer it this way. There is little aquatic vegetation in shallow water for the juvenile fish to hide.

A saumon de fontaine - brook trout was caught in this beautiful valley reaching 57cm. Stocked by the angling association in preference to the large chub that are present.

Now AAPPMA, Gaule Antrainaise – a local angling association have created two catch and release fly-fishing stretches to complement 5 artificially created trout spawning grounds -12 in total and a 500 m canalised fish nursery located in an arm off the river Loysance. A parcours de pêche no-kill sytetch has been created to teach anglers how to fly-fish and a second - parcours no-kill salmonidés roughly 2 km long 5 m wide, the downstream part is deep and slow the upstream part is shallow and fast. The river can be fished with a fly from Antrain up to Moulin du Champinel.

In December you might witness salmon spawning as you walk along bank-side paths. In all the local angling clubs have restored 120 km of banks.

Fly-fishing only stretches: stretch 1. Fish from downstream of the pont de la D97 – roadbridge: until 200 metres upstream of the moulin De Guémorin, in vicinity of Vieux Vy S/Couesnon. Brown, brook and rainbow trout are present. Stretch 2: 1.2 km from downstream of the moulin de Quincampoix: at. Rimou. Brown trout present. Rainbow trout can be caught from the first Saturday in May. Wading only is allowed from the first Saturday in May. Stretch 3. Fish from the moulin du Houx near St-Marc s/ Couesnon downstream to the moulin de Mézières: near Mézières s/Couesnon. Brown trout are present, 1-bag limit for rainbow trout.

More fly-fishing only stretches: river Loysance, fish from Meiderouet upstream, to the moulin des Landelles downstream at the town of St Ouen la Rouérie. River Loysance, from the pont de la D97 upstream, to the moulin de la Chattier situated downstream at the town of St Ouen la Rouérie,

The **étang de la Sablonnière** in Bonnemain. Fly-fishing with two flies maximum is allowed entering from the bank wearing waders, all year round Saturdays, Sundays and Mondays, €10 surcharge for those anglers who wish to use 1-bag limit for rainbow trout. Catch and release is free.

To fish from a boat on the Vilaine River between Cesson and Redon, the Canal d'Ille-et-Rance, and on the plans d'eau de la Bézardière, Hédé, Bazouges S/s Hédé, Boulet, Villemorin et Ouée, ask for permission from the Service Navigation de l'Equipement Tel, 0299592060.

There is no salmon fishing permitted at present in 2006, but please check yourselves with the départemental angling federation, their contact details are given at the start of the section.

Brown trout, rainbow trout and brook trout season runs from 11th March through 17th September. 6-bag limit, 23cm minimum size. Sea trout – 35cm. Salmon – 50cm.

Angling licences: Carte vacances, valid from 1st June to 17th September for 15 consecutive days – €36, Carte Journalière, available from 1st June to 17th September – €8, Carte Jeune – €32 for trout and pike fishing or €5 for coarse angling with one rod, Carte dispense adult – covers pensioners, 1 rod limit – €10. Carte Complète – 65 plus €16.50: if you want to fish in other départements. Salmon and sea trout supplementary tax costs €33.50.

COTES-D'ARMOR (22)

Didier Portanguen an expert local angler gives the reader a good account of his number one river the Gouët located in Cotes-D'Amor.

"The rivers are more suited to trout and salmon in the west of the département where the rivers have granite bedrock. The rivers to the east run through shale that creates a lower water table and where banks become degraded.

There are plenty of trout present. Their numbers are kept high through stocking, poor spawning grounds and dams preventing natural migration upstream that in turn prevents natural reproduction. These stockings have stopped for the past 5 years because they are viewed as detrimental to the welfare of natural fish stocks.

The river Gouët is 45km long. It begins at Haut-Corlay and flows on a granite bed. This is a fly angler's paradise. The river can be divided into three sections. The upstream part until Quintin drains an agricultural area with lots of streams. The channels average 3 m across with a gentle gradient.

The middle section flows from Quintin to the retenue de St-Barthélémy - Etang du Gouët. From Quintin the channel alternates between meanders and faster runs. It is joined by two lovely tributaries the ruisseau du Pas and the ruisseau de St-Germain.

The downstream part is situated at Ste Anne du Houlin. The barrage de St-Barthélémy was built in 1977 reaching 45 m in height. Today the lake is a victim of eutrophication –fertilizer run off from farms causes weed growth that reduces oxygen levels in the water, trout cannot tolerate these conditions and the river just supports coarse fish. As well the defective fish ladder prevents any fish movement. Downstream the river continues towards the sea to Légué where it evolves into a port basin with a lock that inhibits migratory fish.

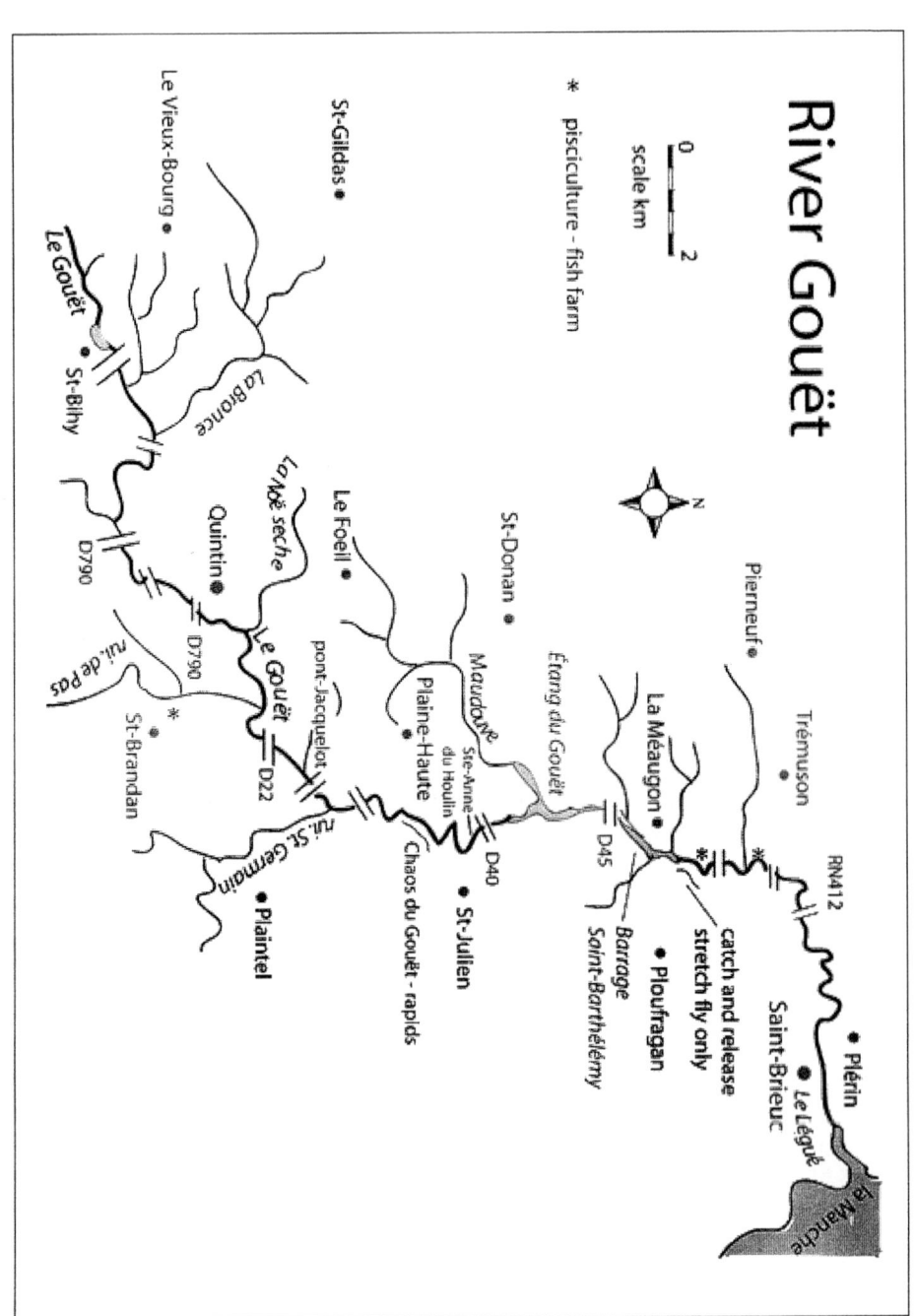

This river is classified as supporting salmon and sea trout, but they are only if rarely found in the lower stretches. In 1953 10-12 salmon annually but with no fish ladders could go no further than the barrage de Méaugon. In spring 2000 2 salmon were caught but the indigenous salmon population remains weak. Despite some salmon parr being released at the source by: source Trieux the spawning grounds are not in good enough to sustain reproduction.

The trout fishing is excellent. Starting upstream the first good stretch is between the étang de Saint-Bihy and Quintin. The narrow channel has a sandy bottom contains a good population of wary trout. When mayflies hatch evenings are very good. A short rod 6-7 feet will suffice.

The middle reaches offer the most interesting stretches. Below Quintin among meandering channels deep holes prove suitable spots to cast a wet fly lure. Here danica – mayfly hatchings are often huge. Several private land estates prohibit access but there are several kilometres of good public stretches to make up for this. Trout density is excellent. A 7-8 foot rod is a good choice. The average channel width is not more than 6 m. Accesses are easy and there are no noisy roads to disturb the tranquility.

Downstream of the Pont de Jacquelot the flow increases and 2 km further downstream it becomes a torrent in a gorge then forms a plan d'eau. The channel widens a little at this stage. A longer rod can gain access with a dry fly to the lee of the granite boulders on a short drift. Hare's ear and red sedge imitation fly lures work well later on in the season. The river is easy to read even when fish stop rising. In spite of the large towns of Brieuc-Quintin there is plenty of wild-river to explore.

The last stretch from the barrage de St-Barthelemy to the estuary is also interesting. High banks box the channel in it's an urban environment. In addition the flow is regulated. Large sea trout were caught here and brown trout reaching 35cm were often caught. The situation deteriorated 10 years ago probably due to the poor water quality in the reservoir. However some brown trout in excess of 5-60cm have spawned in this downstream stretch. The technique of nymphing where fly lures are attached to the main line using droppers is effective, but larger fish in the struggle has often broken anglers' lines.

The AAPPMA of St-Brieuc-Quintin-Binic manages the river basin. There is a parcours mouche no-kill – 600m long catch and release fly-fishing only stretch starting from below the barrage de St-Barthélémy downstream to the remains of the old dam. In spring last season one angler landed 7 trout in excess of 1 kg using a nymph imitation fly lure. The biggest trout so far has measured 56cm. There is a fly-fishing school operating here.Sea trout and salmon sometimes find their way here."

Minimum trout size is 20cm upstream of the étang de Quintin and 23cm downstream.

The **river Trieux situated** to the northwest above Guingamp is one of the best salmon rivers in France it supports an excellent wild brown trout population and welcomes sea trout. It is 44 km long and between 3 m and 12 m wide. Fishing is particularly easy parallel with the D 787 road. Plésidy has a picnic area. There is a 5-bag limit: for trout.

Next valley to the west is the **Jaudy River**. This is an excellent place to catch salmon, sea trout and brown trout. The course is 44 km long and 3 m –12 m wide. Knowledge of the tides is useful and the downstream reaches are more suited to fly-fishing than spinning or au toc.

The **river Léguer** situated further to the west in vicinity of Lannion is one of the biggest rivers in the département. It is a famous salmon river. It is 59 km long and 6 m –20 m wide. There are also plenty of trout to catch. There is a fly-fishing only stretch called the-parcours de mouche du Losser. Caught trout average between 20 cm and 25cm. 3 local angling clubs based at Lannion, Belle-Isle En Terre, Pontrieuc have succeeded from the angling federation and to fish their stretches you will need to contact them directly.

Some good trout rivers all classified in 1st category.

River Ninian situated to the southwest. 20 km long 2 m –5 m wide. Try catching wild brown trout that average 25cm using a short fly rod.

River Oust at Bosméléac. 60 km long 3 m –12 m wide.

River Lié situated in the south to the middle just east of the river Oust. 70 km long 3 m –12 m wide. Excellent for brown trout fishing.

Tributaries worth investigating for fishing include the ruisseaux de Petit Valérien, Ardillets, Léry and Penhouët.

River Blavet situated in the south. Fly-fishing is good at St Roc – Plouguernevel. Au toc - bait fishing is popular at Toul Goulic near Lanrivan where there are plenty of trout. Acid nature of the water prevents fish from exceeding 30cm. However certain swims downstream from the barrage de Guerlédan are well known for giving up trout in excess of 50cm. Average caught trout size is 25cm.

River Hyrère is situated to the southwest. 30km long: in this département, 6 m –12 m wide. Easy access from the D 787 road: that runs parallel along its course. Lots of lovely good size trout. May is the best time to visit. After lunch spoon lures can create havoc. There is a beautiful parcours de mouche – catch and release fly-fishing only stretch at a place known as Kerbaguet – Callac.

River Rance situated to the southeast. Excellent for trout fishing around secteurs de Chaos – rapids: in vicinity of Lanrelas and Quémelin. There are beautiful places to fish around Mérillac and Langourla.

River Arguenon is 64 km long and 1 m –3 m wide. Average caught trout measures 25cm. Trout over 40cm are caught upstream of the lac de Jugon. Immediately north of Jugon les Lacs there are facilities for anglers with **restricted mobility**. A tributary the river Quillory supports wild brown trout in excess of 30cm if the angler heads of the beaten path. There is a parcours de pêche – fly-fishing only catch and release stretch situated in the vicinity of Plénée but it's a bit technical. This often means that the stetch has restricted casting because of nearby trees and dense undergrowth. In this case chest waders are a good way of navigating the channel without re entering the river.

River Ic is situated just east of the river Trieux. It's only 19 km long and 2 m –5 m wide. The stretch ends at Binic. It supports a god population of wild brown trout and often some nice sea trout. Minimum size for brown trout is 20cm except downstream of Camet where the limit is 23cm.

River Leff is a tributary of the river Trieux. 58 km long: and between 2 m and 16 m wide. Pretty parcours de pêche de mouche - fly-fishing only stretch is located at Lanvolon next to the Moulin de Lanvolon – mill.

River Gouëssant in the centre of the département: situated east of Pommeret. Trout fishing is permitted upstream from Lamballe. 61 km long, 1 m –8 m wide. Average caught trout measured 25cm. There is good trout fishing in vicinity of the étang de St Trimoël.

A few lakes

Etang de Beaucours, 1st category situated by St Nicholas de Pelem. It is 2 ha in area and 2 m deep. 1-rod only. 5-bag limit. Day tickets are issued from the second Saturday in March through third Sunday in September. There are regular trout stockings.

Etang Nuef situated near St Connan. 1st category: 8 ha 1 m –3 m deep 1-rod limit. Fly-fishing only from bank or boat. Trout often exceed 3 kg. Once a fortnight spinning is allowed. 2-bag limit. Boat hire contact Tel, 0296681540. Annual licence just for this lake costs €25. Day tickets and angling licences are available from: Passion Pêche Bretagne – tackle shop at Guingamp, Fédération de pêche, Boulevard Arago at St Brieuc, and on site at the lake at weekends and public holidays.

Etang de la Rivière situated near to Haut Corlay. 6 ha 1st category, 1 m-2 m deep, 1-rod limit. A specialist large pike lake. There is good access.

For more information contact: Fédération des Côtes d'Armor pour la pêche et la protection aquatique 66, bd Arago BP 4209 - 22004 St Brieuc- Tel. 02 96 68 15 40 Fax, 02 96 68 15 41

Angling licences

Carte Tax Complète €71
Carte Vacanes €30 fishing for 15 consecutive days from June through September all over France
Carte Jeune 15- €25 10-16 years old
Carte découverte €5 under 10's
Carte Journalière €10
Le timbre halieutique EHGO €16.5 permits fishing in 60 other départements in France
Taxe Grands Salmonidés Migrateur €33.5 obligatory to fish for salmon and sea trout

Maison de la Pêche - sells the angling licence and is a fly-fishing school thay are based at:

Sébastien Juvaux
2 rue des Grands Moulins
22 270 Jugon-les-Lacs
Tel, 0296506004 – Fax, 0296506026
Email: maisondelapeche@wanadoo.fr
www.maisondelapeche22.com

Angling licences may be purchased from the following establishments

Belle Isle en Terre: Christophe Morise, Le Bar'tin Pêcheur, 10 Rue Saint Jacques à Belle Isle
Broons: Laguiton Fleuriste et Articles de pêche, rue de la Barrière 22 250 Broons Tel, 0296847379
Callac: Pierre Cazoulat, Le Comptoir de Campagne, rue des Portes 22 160 Callac Tel, 0296455106
Caulnes: Gigafouille 82 Route de Dinan 22 350 Caulnes Tel, 0296838485
Châtelaudren: Le Maître Lucienne, Bar Alimentation 22 170 Boqueho Tel, 0296739220
Dinan: Patrick Azalot - Pêche et chasse - 17 Rue Carnot 22100 Dinan Tel, 0296392037
Guingamp: Passion Pêche Bretagne 12 place St Sauveur Tel, 0296400833
Lamballe: Graineterie LeMarchande - Place du Marché 22 400 Lamballe Tel, 0296310377
Lannion: Armurerie Le Laouenan- 2 rue de la Mairie Lannion: Maël-Carhaix Bar-Loto La Fontaine, 19 Rue de la Gare 22 340 Mael Carhaix Tel, 0296246321
Moncontour: Bar La Vieille Tour 1 Rue Notre Dame 22 510 Moncontour Tel, 0296735382
Plancoët: Café des sports, le bourg 22 250 Matignon Tel, 0296410234
St Brieuc Quintin Binic: Armor Pêche - 5 bis Rue Dol 22 410 Saint Quay Portrieux Tel, 0296704034

FINISTÈRE (29)

Marcel Madec a local angler describes his favourite river the Jarlot River in the département Finistère.

"The Jarlot is the second river to pass through the town of Morlaix. It joins the Queffleuth River below the town hall to form the river Morlaix below the écluse – town weir. It's a small river roughly 20 km long beginning in wetlands between Plougonven and Lannéanou. There are deep and shallow runs, rapids and slower wider parts. The course ends in a pretty valley. Average channel width is 5 m –7 m, and it's quite shallow. Fly anglers will want to visit from June onwards when mayfly hatches lure fish to the surface to feed on the insects. A 7 ½ to 8-foot rod is suitable for dry fly fishing. A bit longer: for wet fly. Select dark coloured fly lures using small hooks size 14, 16 or 18.

Stretch 1: from Morlaix at the gare de Coatelan – train station. The channel is bordered by the chemin de fer Morlaix-Carhaix - old railway line. There are plenty of trout: averaging 20cm -23cm. Some occasional salmon and exceptionally: sea trout. Downstream reach: pont de l'ancienne piscine – old swimming pool bridge by the Morlaix sign – confluence with the Tromorgan. 800 m long, parking is available. Water inlet above the bridge, 5 m –6 m wide average depth is 1 m. Some deep pools and a few old mills. Fast runs through to semi-torrent. Tricky wading conditions although waders are essential: and quite slippery. Many smaller trout: in deeper pools and calmer water and occasionally: salmon. Although it is a pleasant venue few choose to fish here.

2nd stretch: from the Pont-Noir to the Moulin Marant. 1.2 km long: it takes 3-4 hours t offish the whole stretch. Parking at the Pont Noir situated 200 m away towards the Hermitage. Take a path on the right. The river is found below. 1st reach: is a beautiful meadow situated below the Hermitage. There is a good head of trout in the deepest bends of the three meanders. 2nd reach: 200 m long, narrower and very woody. Some interesting narrow deep pools reward a good casting technique. 3rd reach: two lovely meadows, the first is left to grow and offers good fishing along its meandering course. The second field offers easier access and it flows faster. All the tempting liars are by the bank. Reach 4: lots of trees make it difficult to fish. This is not helped by barbed wire. The best swims are 50 m before the bridge. Anglers should return by the old

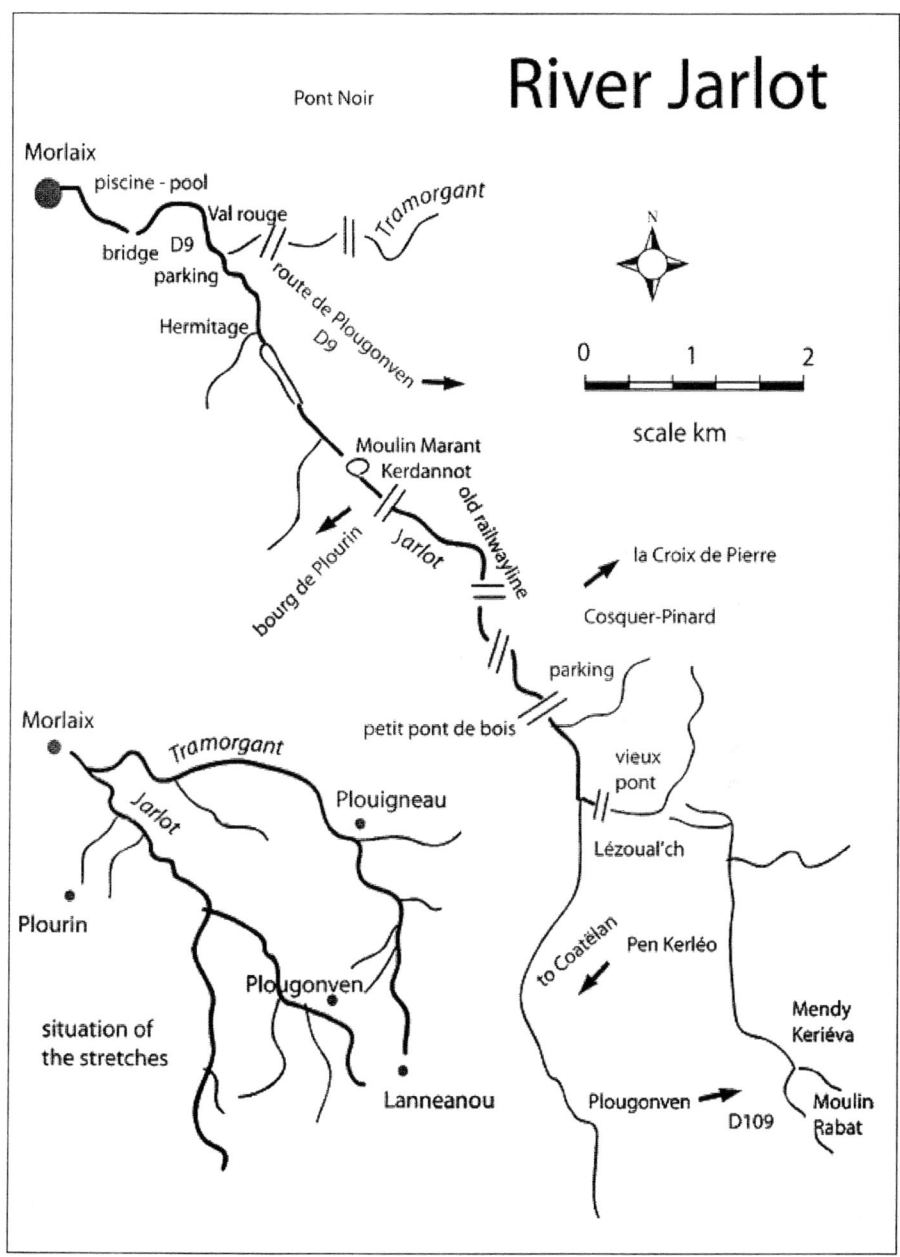

railway. It's good fishing from the end of May till to the start of July when May flies hatch. During this period afternoons are better than at dusk. The fish have a pretty patterned bronze livery.

3rd stretch: from Moulin Marant to the route de la Croix de Pierre. 2.2 km long, 5-6 hours fishing time. The river is wildest on this reach. The most difficult to fish: and the least visited by anglers. The shallow water flows quickly and branches into many smaller channels: that are full of visible rocks where fishing requires a technical approach. Effort made is compensated by the get away from it all type of atmosphere. Wading is required to reach some swims. The small trout are hard fighters and the best time to fish is the second half of June.

4th stretch: from the Croix de Pierre to Lezoual'ch. From the Croix de Pierre head towards Plourin 1 km ahead turn left by the pedestrian crossing and park up close to the bailiff's house then walk 200 m through the wood down to the river. The stretch is 1 km long and considered an easy fish it contains rapids and calm water. There are lots of trout ranging from 20-22cm, there is light angling pressure, and fishing is best at the mayfly hatch.

5th stretch: from Lézoual'ch to Kerléva. From Coatélan: head towards Lézoual'ch. Park up after the bridge as shown on map IGN point 86. As you progress upstream past the bridge three different meadows present themselves. Fish the deep pools by the bridge at the first field. The bend at the top of the reach is worth investigating. Bordering a wood the second meadow is not worth fishing. The last field starting from the small wooden bridge is the most interesting to fish. A series of small pools contain some lively trout caught on mayfly imitation fly lures in May through June. It's one of the best spots on the river, wading is a real pleasure.

6th stretch: from Kerléva to Moulin Rabat. 700 m stretch. The channel is a large stream; fishing is mainly to the well-marked pools. The best looking swims are located 100 m after the tunnel. At the head of the stretch below the ferme de Mendy-Kerléva farm the channel and supports lots of insect larvae especially caddis along its meandering course. Slow current over a sandy bed encourage mayfly hatchings. Dense aquatic vegetation conceals the angler's approach but embarrasses their casting. Occasional fallen trees offer excellent boltholes."

Maps IGN: Morlaix 616O (parcours1, 2&, 3), Morlaix 616 E (parcours3, 4 &5).

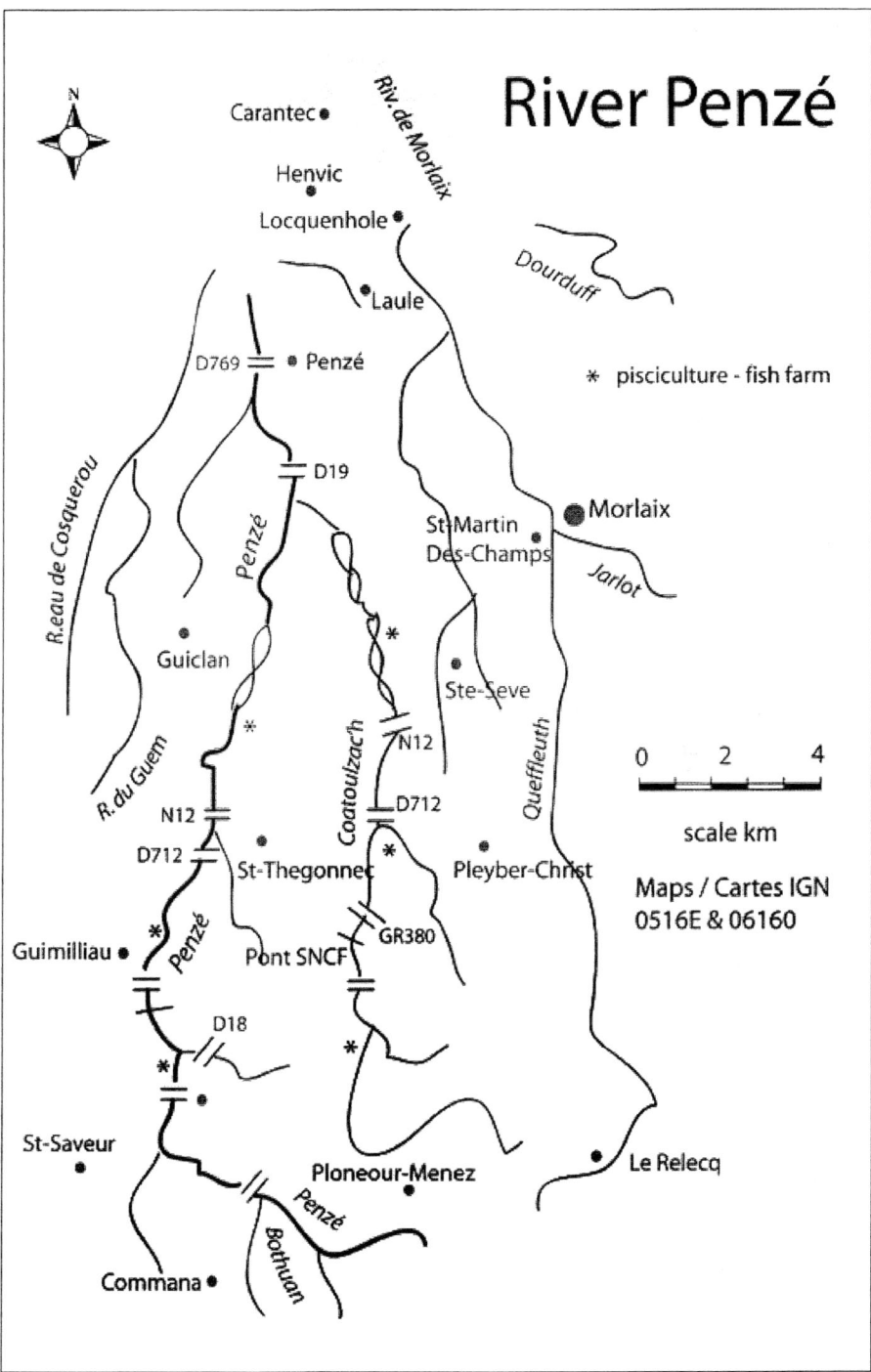

River Penzé

Louis Coat a respected local angler has the following to say.

"The Penzé is one of the best trout rivers in Brittany and it certainly offers the highest average size of fish. Plenty of trout from 28-30cm. Specimens reach 50cm especially in the middle and lower stretches from Saint to Thégonnec.

From June to July in evening time, 50% of fish captures exceeded 30cm, 20% exceed 34cm and 10% reach past 36cm.

At other times the river can appear empty. From 2003 a 7 km stretch on the upstream reaches above Saint-Thégonnec was restored for the enjoyment of fly anglers. Downstream stretches between Penzé and the Pont de Penzé have been cleaned up. Creating new opportunities for the salmon fly angler.

The river contains sea trout and salmon as well as trout. Previously the lower reaches had proved largely inaccessible to fly-fishermen.

At Penzé there is a 10-bag limit 20cm minimum size, further upstream at Elorn there is a 6-bag limit 23cm minimum size. A small tributary the Coatoulzac River joins the Penzé downstream. It is less fickle than the Penzé and anglers will always find trout there. The fishare smaller but about average size for Brittany. This river used to give up brown trout up to 75cm."

The département of Finistère contains 25 local angling clubs and 7,000 licensed anglers. The area contains 4500 km of 1st category rivers. i.e. those that contain salmon, sea trout, brook trout and rainbow trout. Fishing for Atlantic salmon is this département's spcciality. The big money goes on in spring when the largest salmon attempt their climb up Finistères rivers. In June arrive castillons – smaller salmon that have experienced one year at sea."

Apart from famous salmon rivers: like the Aulne, Ellé, Aven, Goyen, Elorn, Mignonne, Aber Vrac'h, Penzé and Douron. The réservoir de St Michel situated in the interior has some outstanding trout fishing. The annual season ticket for this reservoir costs €18 for locals and €28 for every one else, in addition to the angling licence. €13 for a day ticket: without angling licence or €10 for those anglers in procession of an angling licence.

For more information contact: Fédération du Finistère pur la Pêche
4, Allée Loeiz herrieu, zone de Kéradennec
– 29000 Quimper
Tel, 0298103420 Fax, 0298102208
Email: fedepeche29@wanadoo.fr

Season for brown trout, grayling and brook trout is from 11th March through 17th September. Same period applies to rainbow trout in salmon rivers. Elsewhere they can be fished for all year.

Angling licences: Carte complète – €69 annual licence that permits fishing all waters managed by the département angling federation including all lakes stocked with trout, an additional €10 is charged if anglers want to fish in neighbouring départements, carte vacances, issued from June through September – €30, carte juene, under 16's – €21, Carte Découverte, under 12's, 50% discount on école de pêche angling schools– €8, carte journalière – €10, Pass Pêche 29 is an annual season ticket for anglers from outside the département allows fishing in all 22 reciprocal Finistère waters not including réservoir de St Michel.

To fish for salmon the Taxe Migrateurs is obligatory it costs €33.50.

Websites for angling: in Finistére
http://pecher-saint-renan.org covers St Renan area
www.elorn-aappma.com covers lac de Drenne on the river Élorn at Landerneau

Websites for fishing in Brittany

www.invfmr.or good for French fly lures
http://aappmaelorn.chez-alice.fr website of local angling club AAPPMA L'Elorn
http://aappmaquimperle.fr website for Quimperlé

Local angling club websites
Breizh Etel Club Mouche en Mer: http://www.e-monsite.com/becmm/

Le Club Mouche de l'Odet: http://clubmouchelodet.free.fr
Club Français du refendu: http://club.fr.refendu.free.fr/
Les Moucheurs Nantais: http://lesmoucheursnantais.free.fr/
Club de pêche de Notre-Dame de Bury: http://naturepeche.free.fr/

The Quimper area

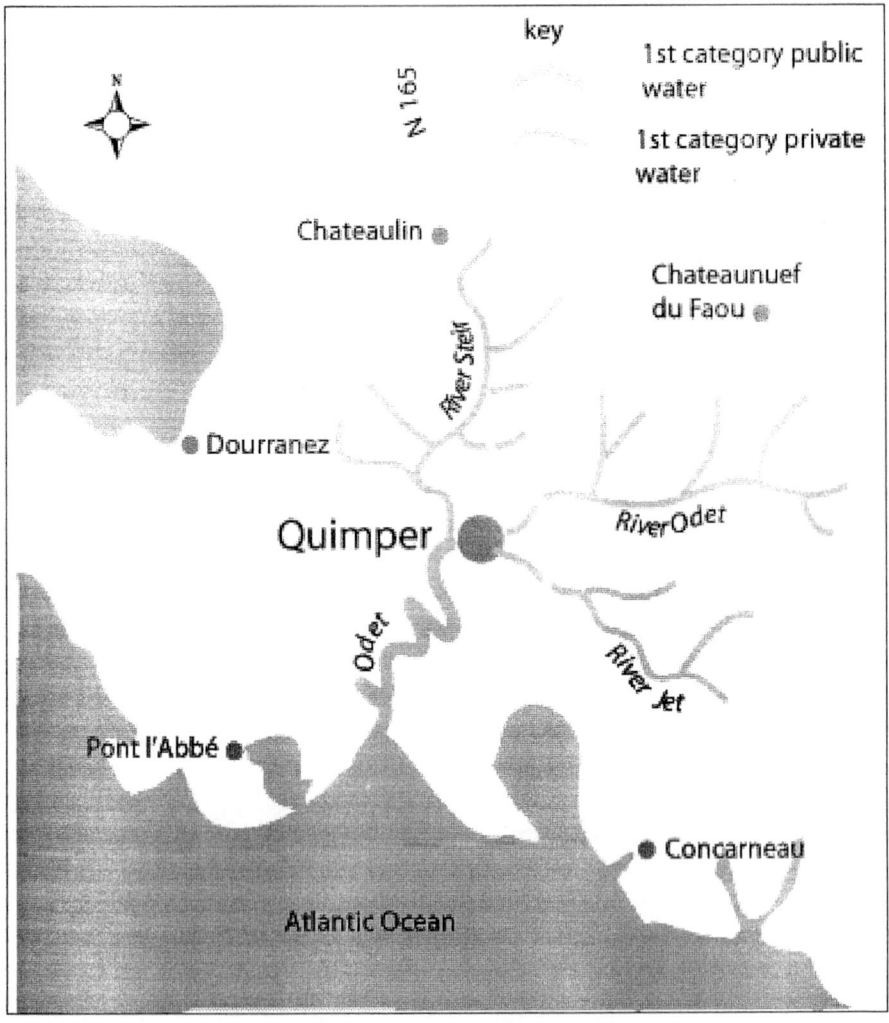

Jean Jacques Le Moal an expert local fly angler describes three favourite trout fishing rivers in the lovely countryside surrounding Quimper.

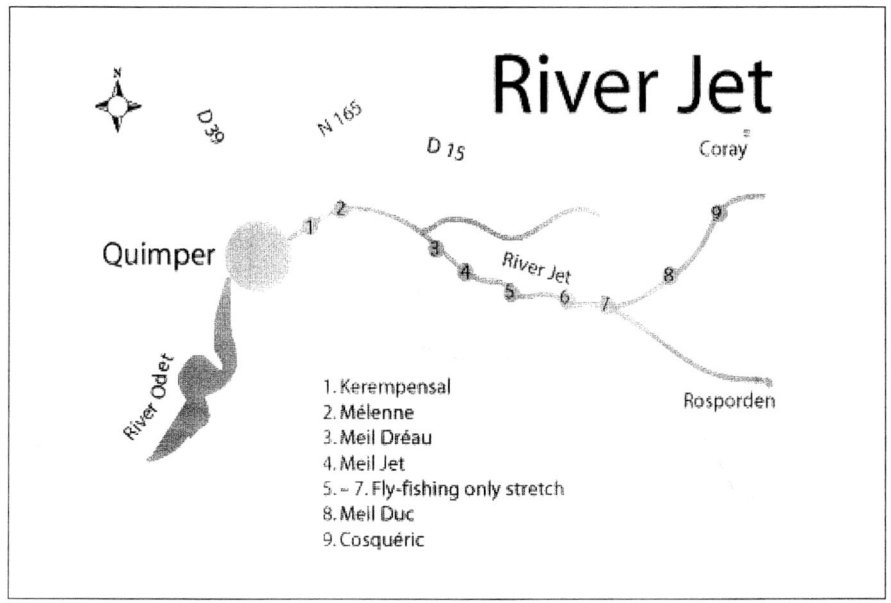

1. "The River Jet is the slowest and deepest of the rivers around Quimper. It takes its source close to Coray, crosses Elliant then after a course of roughly 30 km joins the Odet River at Quimper. It is a splendid river easily accessible and suitable for fly-fishing along its banks from Quimper to Elliant.

Access is via a number of bridges on route. One way from Quimper to Elliant is along the D115 for about 5 km and to a place called Kerdiles access the channel by descending from the Trois Moulins restaurant.

Downstream from the bridge, the river presents a rather slow reach alternating between currents and large pools that are very welcoming to a wet fly at the start of the season. Its hollow banks shelter pretty trout that will attack a train of three flies correctly presented. In the deep holes you will be able to sometimes surprise salmon in a vacant moment but anglers can also attract the lamprie that migrate up the river from spring onwards.

Upstream a small rod from 7 to 8 feet is recommended. The course is more technical and the abundant vegetation sees mayfly hatchings and more colourful insects. Short accurate casting is required. The trout are smaller than those found further downstream but can be more numerous and there are often surprises.

A second stretch is by Saint Yvi heading towards Rosporden make a left turn to the church then to continue straight, passing under the railway bridge and park up close to the next bridge spanning the river. Here the fly-fishing stretch is 1 km long and is reserved for fly-fishing only from 1st May on a catch and release basis.

This pretty course meanders through meadows and woods and presents the angler with alternating deep pools and faster current, the channel bed is sandy here. A local fly-fishing club called Club Mouche de l'Odet maintains the stretch. It is easily fishable with a fly lure. A rod of 8 feet, number 4-5 line, and a monofilament leader less than 3 pounds breaking strain.

Let us not forget that the fly will be chosen according to circumstances a Meil Poul is a variant of the Pont Audemer, a Prof K, a Cul de Canard or of course a sedge fly imitation lure. Add to that a good amount of skill a bit of inspiration and some luck and you will experience a lovely day fishing along the riverbank.

A third stretch is situated on the same road continuing towards Elliant stop close to the bridge at the bottom of the village of Cosquéric. There, two possibilities await you: either descend the river wading casting a nymph fly lure or descend without fishing for roughly 1.5 km – 2 km then head upstream casting a dry fly. The stretch has difficult access and you will meet few fishermen. The narrowness of the channel makes this stretch more technical. A short rod, accurate casting, hold your nerve. Success depends on it. The trout although less put upon than elsewhere are not stupid.

The river Jet is a difficult river that requires much humility. Good days alternate with quieter periods. Its hollow banks accomodate beautiful fish with perfect hiding places. A 30cm specimen is not unheard of.

Wandering grayling paint a picture and buttercups crowd the water in May making it sometimes difficult to present a fly. From the start of the season to half way through April a three fly lure presentation cast over to the far bank and over submerged obstacles will prove effective. On the end fly lure choose a golden head nymph – Nivirit type, in the middle a Pallaretta and a jumper a Garsabic – March Brown.

From the second fortnight of April if the water is in order you will be able to cast with a Prof K or a sedge fly lure Pont Quéau. The calmest stretches will be covered using a no hackle fly lure or a small dark Cul de Canard. Sometimes a Mayfly hatch will lure the big'ns to the surface. But do not forget, the Jet is a river that is earned. Persevere and it will be its own reward where one morning there is the chance of spotting otters or a nimble red squirrel hurdling branches. Who said that happiness does not exist?"

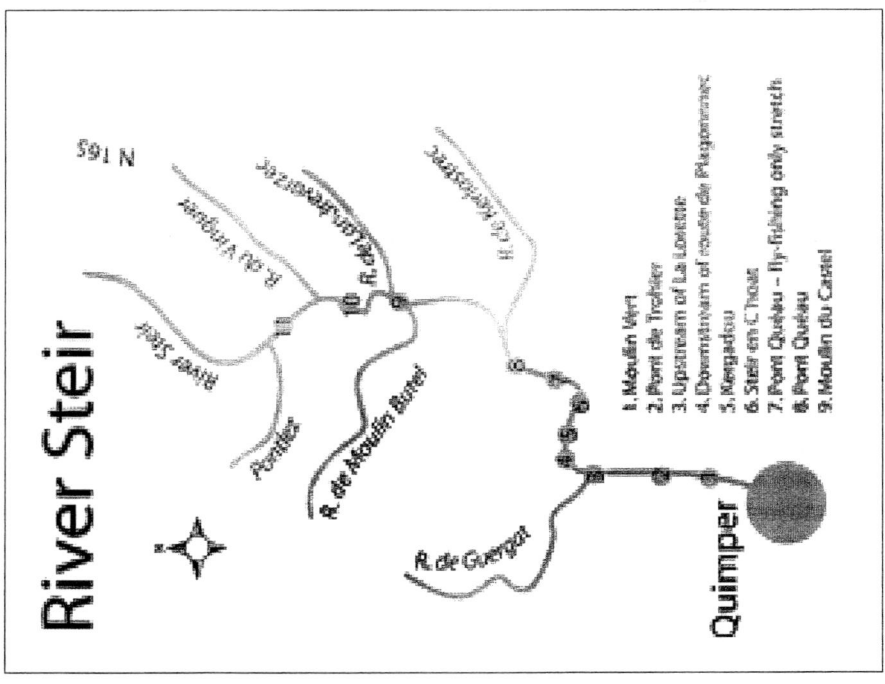

2. "The Steïr River along with along with the Jet is the principal affluent of Odet River and they empty into the Odet at Quimper. It is 28 km long; beginning near Cast and its basin has a catchment area of 202 km ^{2}. Just like the Jet and Odet, the Steïr has its parcours mouche no kill – catch and release stretch situated from approximately 1 km upstream of the place called Pont-Quéau. One can however consider it regrettable that this course is exclusive fly-fishing only starting from mid-April. The A.A.P.P.M.A. of Quimper – local angling club publishes a colour

booklet, available by simple request from local tackle shops, containing all of the information useful for the fisherman e.g. fly-fishing stretches, rules and regulations and maps.

The river Steïr has been the object, just like the whole of the réseau hydrographique Quimpérois, of a policy of selective cleaning for several years. Obstacles removed in order to allow the natural flow of the river while preserving the river's vegetation favourable to the food for trout.

The Steïr being used as supply water with a good part going to Quimper, one will note the absence of fish farms and polluting industry on its banks. However, the presence of many agricultural farms increases the nitrate rate (eutrophication) considerably. An increase: from 26ml/l in 1977 to 36 ml/l in 1997. Brown trout are the dominant fish.

For 4 years, the A.A.P.P.M.A. of Quimper has practised a patrimonial management that implies the total absence of stocking with fish fry or adult trout releases. Also eels, lamprey, minnows, chub, loaches and dace are allowed to thrive. Creating a balanced fish environment. The salmon is also present, 600 spawning grounds are counted along the course of the Steïr.

The fisherman knowing how to be discrete will be able to observe a large variety of animal species in depth of valley, in the zones known as conservatoires far away from farmer's fields. One can encounter here muskrats and their predator the mink, the weasel, bats and squirrels. The vipers, slow worms, salamanders and frogs suffer from the impoverishment of the medium but buzzards, sparrow hawks, and tawny owls are quite common. At the edge of water, martin pêcheur - kingfisher and the grey wagtail nest between the stones of the old mills.

From its source near Cast, the Steïr River, on the local angling club stretch called A.A.P.P.M.A. of Quéménéven is like many Breton brooks, a pipi d'eau – streak of piss circulating through the meadows and the thickets. Only the fishermen with the worm at the start of the season or the insect in summer wet their line here. It is only starting from the road connecting Quémeméven to its station that the river becomes practicable with the fly lure.

A few hundred meters upstream of the bridge, the river flows through an open meadow. 5 meters wide over a sandy bottom, it is the sector where you can prick a trout with a dry fly lure at the start of the season. This section of river is best avoided in windy weather.

Downstream from the bridge and until the D56 road connecting Landrévarzec with Plogonnec, the Steïr is narrower and deeper. The banks in many places are quite excavated at their base, providing very interesting boltholes for trout.

The banks have many trees and bushes making casting from the bank with a fly lure problematic. For the fisherman in waders provided with a rod of 6 or 7 feet, the tracking of these fish little requested by the moucheurs – fly fishermen will bring an unquestionable pleasure.

Downstream from this sector, managed by local angling club A.A.P.P.M.A. de Quimper, the profile changes little, the river widens slightly, it allows the use of a rod of 8 feet. The meadows of Keréfren and des Salles make it possible to cast from the bank using a wet fly lure with a good chance of success.

The fly-fishing stretch found downstream from these meadows begins, upstream boundary, a little above the high-tension lines and ends by the railway bridge upstream of Pont-Quéau. The small currents succeed calm areas and the zones rich in vegetation but less invasive than those on the Jet and Odet. The meadows of Pont-Quéau propose to us major stretches attended regularly by the saumoniers until the beginning of the summer.

Downstream and until the D39 road connecting Quimper to Plogonnec, the Steïr widens and the diversity of the swims makes it possible to please most anglers. Downstream from the Plogonnec road, the river describes a broad loop that ends in a narrow canyon from the top of which one can spot trout and with a little luck salmon. The fishing of this sector is very pleasant and anglers may wish to spend a good few moments without breaking sweat with too much technical casting.

Again downstream, the sectors of la lorette, typlanch, or troheir, remain locations attracting the fly-fisherman, then the Steïr returns to Quimper where it will join the Odet. You will be able to see there as of the beautiful days, mullet between one and six pounds in weight, in tight schools, marsouiner - porpoise along the bank's edge".

Joel Bougain's tackle: rod 6 to 7 feet for the sector upstream 8 feet for the remainder: when wading with a dry fly lure. 9 feet - 9 feet ½ for casting from the bank: with a wet fly lure. Line 4/5 Cuissardes – cycling shorts or pantalon de pêche – fishing trousers. Wading authorized on certain sectors from 1st May.

Fly lures: Palaretta, Garsabic, billes dorées - gilded balls, bibi, tinsel… for wet fly. Meil castel, Pont Quéau, Jo killer, féline killer… for the dry fly lure Nymphe Saywer, Kergadou, Nivirit… for the nymph. * See the fly lure card on our website: www.club-mouche-odet.com

Good value gite accommodation is available for rent at the ferme de Sainte Cécile-Brice – farmhouse, contact Francoise and René Tel, 02989451 or email: r.f.petillon@wanadoo.fr

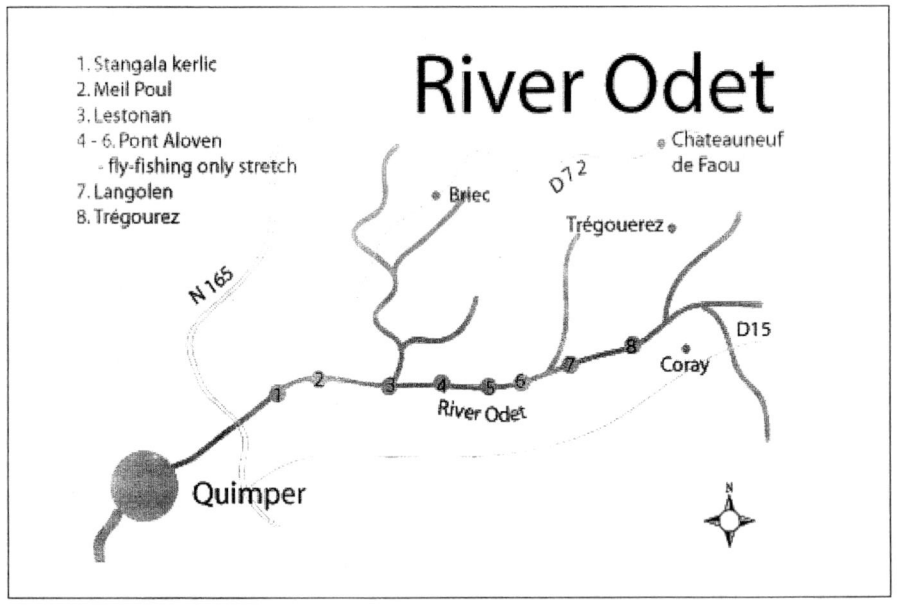

3. "The Odet is longest and most powerful of the Quimper Rivers. Thanks to its confluence with the Steir and the Jet gave to the city the name of Kemper en Breton meaning junction. From the various bridges that span the river one can spot mullet in petty thieving and of course

some trout that profit forever from a fishing ban in the town centre. Thereafter, beyond the law courts that are the limits of saline water the Odet widens and meandering enters the Gorges des Vire shortly before emptying into the Atlantic Ocean between Bénodet and Sainte Navy.

The estuary of the Odet is not only full of mullet sea bass also swim up with each tide. The fly-fishing amateur will find there an ideal playground here to test the many fly lure imitations of shrimp, alevins – fish fry and other streamers constituting the panoply of the sea bass angler.

Not being a specialist in sea bass fishing I propose to you to stroll along the banks of Odet while starting from its source. Born in the black mountains in the middle of Brittany Odet begins close to Roudouallec. Its 56 km's are a treat for the fly-fisherman. Rather wise on the first two thirds of its course the Odet crosses successively stretches managed by local angling clubs APPMA Leuhan, Tregourez, Coray then Quimper.

The majority of its channel bed consists of sand and gravel. The abrupt banks impose the practice of wading but constitute often-insuperable obstacles when leaving the bsnk is the best option. The abundant watery vegetation present as from May makes some stretches unfishable to the fly lure because the vegetable carpet is so dense.

It is the domain of the trout fat and powerful that knowing their environment perfectly, exploit the least weaknesses of the fisherman and with the least error precipitate in the water buttercups where it is very difficult to dislodge them. Continuing its meanders through meadows and wood we arrive at the parcours mouche de Pont Alouen fly-fishing stretch situated by the D51 road - between Quimper and Coray exit the D15 by the croix St André - crossroads continue for 2 km's and stop by the first bridge.

One kilometre long, this sector is in fact reserved for fishing with the fly lure only from 15th April and wading is authorized there only after 1st May. The current is slow and there are plenty of large fish present. It should be said that food is abundant here as well out of fish forages as in insects of all kinds e.g. mayflies, tricoptères - sedges and baétidés. Trout often exceed 30cm. In the absence of trout rising investigate carefully between the riverweed and the strong current casting from the bank with a sedge roux - russet-red sedge. Downstream the river widens, its channel bed becomes stonier and resembles a mountain torrent while passing through the Gorges du Stangala.

This stretch is accessible from various ways the simplest being as follows: from Quimper head towards Brest, towards the roundabout, zone de Gourvily pass the bridge under the four ways and take the first right, continue for 500 m then with the following crossing on the left, continue for 300 m and park up in the Kerlic car park.

By tuning the ear one can hear the Odet thunder at the bottom of the valley. A small way will carry you to the river. It is a paradise for the fisherman in love with running water. A long rod equipped with a fine line and a bottom of line runs is required.

The fish are numerous there but of a smaller size than further up the Odet. Every water crease line, each rock shelters beautiful mouchetée - trout that will surprise you by their promptness and capacity to play you with rotten tricks. The drifts will be short but precise and the fly lures to select will be visible and buoyant. Sedge chevreuil - Sedge roedeer, araignée bien fournie - well provided spider.

Think about using felt soles if you want to avoid a forced bath. To fill the waders with a tank full is never a pleasant thing especially at the start of the fishing day. Thereafter the river enters Quimper and fishing is banned throughout the town centre".

Tackle: upstream stretches: a short rod of 7 - 7 ½ feet will enable you to pass everywhere. On the fly stretch and downstream a rod of 8 - 8 ½ feet will hit the spot. The gorges du Stangala will be fished with a long rod, 9-10 feet and a fine line.

Fly lures: for fast water, provided or visible spiders (Meil poul, royal Traun), sedges chevreuil - roe-deer sedge or palmers will enable you to attract the beautiful mouchetées - trout. The slower stretches will be fished with flies of the type No-hackle (Meil castel) or the emergent sedges (féline killer).

Regulations: fly-fishing only, from 15th April on the parcours de Pont Alouen – river stretch. Catch and release. Wading is authorized from 1st

May. Apart from the fly only stretches called parcours mouche, the minimum size is 20cm and bag limit is 10 fish per angler per day.

To view good photographs of all the stretches depicted in the previous four maps visit the website www.club-mouche-odet.com

Click on the banner called Parcours then click through the map for images. Click on the Montage banner to view local fly patterns including good photography illustrating fly tying techniques.

Local expert fishing guide Bruno Joncour offers a taste of his favourite lake. "There are lots of different types of lakes in Finistière, the reservoir St-Michel – map IGN 06170 is situated in the middle of Finistière. The water covers 450 ha and its large size offers another dimension to still water fishing. It's always full of rainbow trout and pike, this lake is full of surprises.

The average catch is between one and two fish per session. Several approaches are possible. From the shore the number of reaches is relatively limited. From a canoe or boat – with electric trolling motor is the best way to fish here. Alternating with wading from the bank.

Tackle: to catch pike a powerful rod is essential to cast the bulky pike fly lures. However anglers can vary the size of line to suite conditions. To catch rainbow trout whilst wading a traditional reservoir rod is sufficient.

Fly lures for pike fishing: fly lures predominately white in colour achieve good results on the plan d'eau de Brennelis. A little tip: to transform a regular fly lure into a popper lure just cut up a foam hair curler into small pieces then place at the front of the fly lure. It's an inexpensive, practicable and effective solution.

Fly lures for catching rainbow trout in a reservoir include black, orange and white streamers. Sedges, chironomes and beetle fly lures."

Bruno is happy to take visitng anglers fly fishing for trout for a day or two and can provide gites accommodation near the river. Email: bjoncour@club-peche.com Tel, 0298666923, mobile – 0681668824 his website address: http://bjpeche.com

CORRÈZE (19)

In this département there are 4,000 km of rivers are classified in 1st and 2nd category and 4,500 ha of retenues hydro-électrique – hydroelectric power dams and lakes.

For more information contact:	Fédération de Pêche de la Corrèze 33 Bis, Place Abbé Tournet – 19000 Tulle Tel, 0555261155 fax, 0555261572 Email: pechecorreze@wanadoo.fr www.peche-correze.com
Where to seek help and additional information?	Brigade du Conseil, Supérieur de la Pêche (C.S.P.) Tel & fax 0555208815.

What type of angling licence do I need?

All the following are defined as Carte de pêche annuelle - annual angling licences.

Carte de pêche avec taxe complète – full angling licence: including carp night fishing, spinning and trout water. 4-rod limit on 2nd category water: 2-rod limit on 1st category water – in special cases. However unless specified there is usually a 1-rod limit on 1st category water. A maximum of 3 flies per line or two artificial baits. Cost is €64 per year.

Carte de pêche Jeune: for anglers under 16 years old. Includes the Club halieutique – reciprocal fishing rights in other départements. Permits the holder to fish in both 1st and 2nd category water employing all methods of angling. Cost is €24 per year.

Carte annuelle and Carte jeune angling licences offer automatic membership of the AAPPMA – half of the cost of the angling licence goes to the national angling federation and qualification for the halieutique – reciprocal arrangement for fishing in other départements.

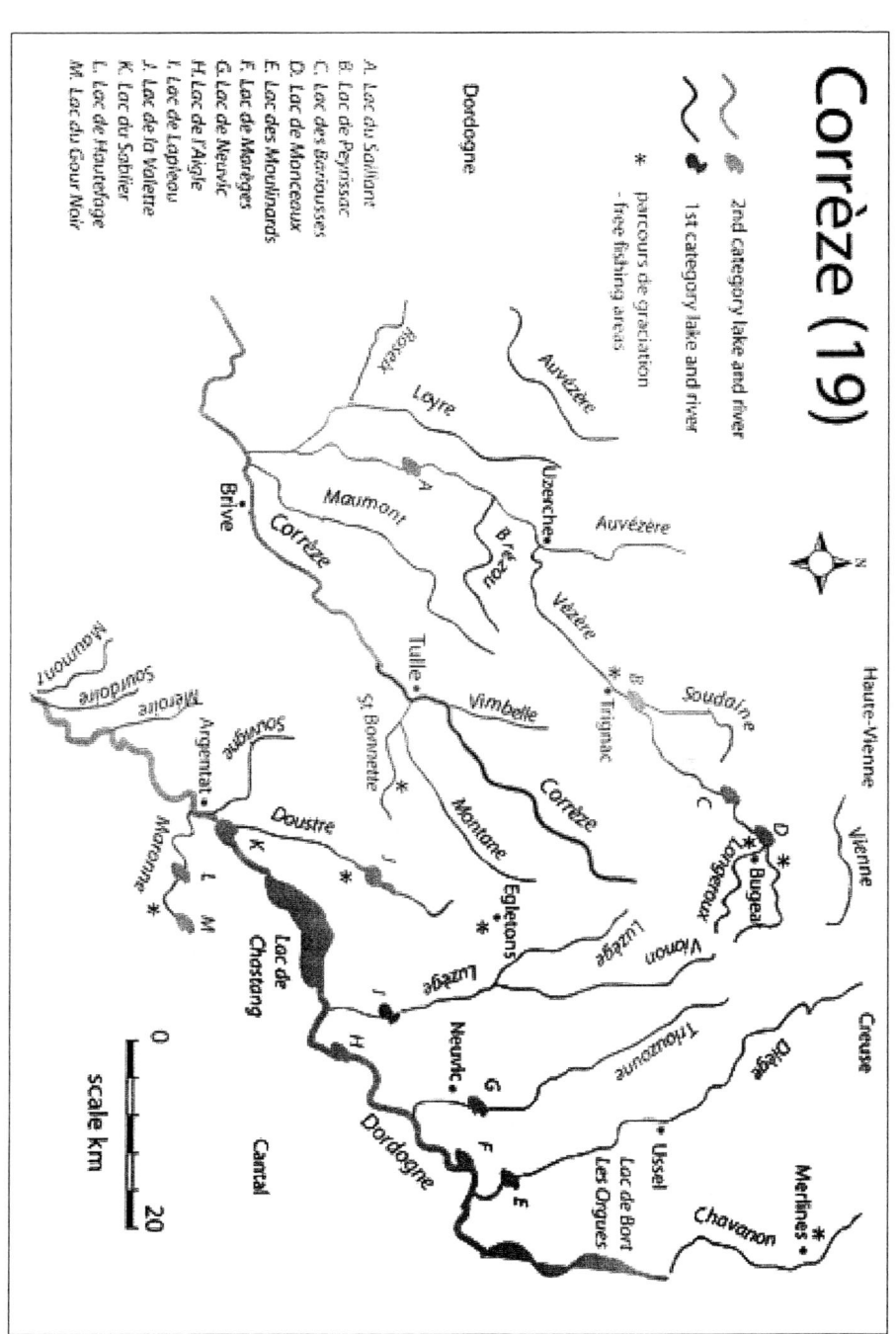

Carte de pêche vacances: valid for 15 consecutive days from 1st June through 15th September. Permits the holder to fish in both 1st and 2nd category water and in all the lakes classified as 1st category within this département; all methods of fishing are permitted. 2-rod limit in 1st category water when fishing for coarse fish, 1-rod limit: when fishing for trout, 4-rod limit on 2nd category water. Cost is €30.

Carte de pêche Exonere: permits all types of fishing except spinning, but does include night fishing and fly-fishing with one rod, on both 1st and 2nd category water. Partners of licence holders qualify. Cost is €15 per year. Children under 16 years old, cost is €2 per year. Pensioners, cost is €15 per year

Carte de pêche journalière: day ticket for individual waters. Cost is €8.

Carte et timbre tax piscicole plan d'eau – since 1992 an angling licence and permission is required to fish lakes that are free where the water exceeds 1 hectare in area. Essentially this permission is required for private lakes not managed by the AAPPMA. The cost of permission is zero but you need to ask for permission from the angling federation.

These different permits allow the angler to fish the parcours de pêche domaine privé – stocked private fishing reserves managed by the AAPPMA and public waters all over France and private waters that have reciprocal arrangements with other AAPPMA's.

Rules and Regulations:

There are no sea trout in this département. Fishing for salmon is banned to increase their chances of re-introduction into the département.

Use of maggots and other insect larvae is banned in 1st category waters. Although there are some 1st category lakes are exceptional to this rule. But in no circumstances can maggots be used in ground bait.

1st category lakes managed by the AAPPMA

Le Coiroux at Aubazine. Poncharal at Vigeoix. Séchemailles at Meymac Ambrugeat. Plan d'eau communal de Peyrelevade. Plan d'eau communal d'Egletons. The use of maggots without ground bait is authorised on these waters. On these waters anglers are allowed to spin and use live and dead baits for trout outside the pike and zander season. But not anywhere else.

No ground bait or hook bait consisting of maggots is permitted on the River Dordogne, downstream of the Barrage EDF du Sablier at Argentat and up to the Pont Beaulieu – RD940.

On the Dordogne River, downstream from the Argentat electricity board dam (barrage EDF d'Argentat), the following fishing techniques and procedures are forbidden: the use of maggots or other insect larvae as bait or ground bait, downstream from the Sablier dam - le Barrage du Sablier, Argentat and as far as the D940 bridge at Beaulieu on the Dordogne river. Down stream from this bridge and as far as the Corrèze border, the use of maggots and larvae bait is allowed but their use as ground bait is forbidden.

The use of the accessory known as bikini - artificial fly trail cast by a weight submerged on the end of the line is banned.

Where salmon and sea trout may exist in a river stretch angling only with one rod is allowed. Only fishing from the bank is allowed. No wading. On these waters only bait fishing is allowed fly-fishing, live and dead baiting and spinning are banned. These waters are described as follows.

Corrèze River downstream of the Pont des Angles, at town of the same name, route 58, up to the confluence with the Vézère. Dordogne River, public water situated downstream of the barrage du Sablier, at Argentat until the end of the Corrèze département. Maronne River, downstream of the barrage de Hautefage, until its confluence with the Dordogne.

Souvigne River, from the pont du chemin départemental n°10 road situated around Forgès: until its confluence with the Dordogne. Vézère, River downstream of the barrage de Peyrissac until the end of the département de la Corrèze.

Minimum fish sizes

American largemouth Black bass are considered a pest in 1st category water, in 2nd category 30cm.
Pike are considered a pest in 1st category water, in 2nd category 60cm.
Grayling in all water: 30cm.
Zander are considered a pest in 1st category water, 2nd category 40cm.
Trout: 1st category, 20cm – 23cm on the River Cère. 2nd category water, 25cm, 30cm on the River Dordogne.

Bag limits: zander and pike – 5 fish. Trout – 1st category water, 10 fish, maximum of 2 grayling. 2nd category water, 5 fish on the River Dordogne, maximum of 2 grayling.

Angling season

Trout: 11th March through 17th September on all water.
Pike: 1st category water, classed as a nuisance fish species but season runs from March through 17th September. 2nd category water: close season from 30th January through 14th May.
Zander: 1st category water, classed as a nuisance fish species but season runs from March through 17th September. 2nd category water, close season runs from 12th March through 13th May.

Other fish species: 1st category, season runs from 11th March through 17th September. 2nd category: all year round.

Anglers can fish from half an hour before sunrise to half an hour after sunset. Times depend on the time of year from a start at 8.30 a.m. to 4.35 p.m. in January to 6.30 a.m. to 7.30 p.m. in July.

1ST Category Waters

Anglers fish mainlyfor brown trout: but also gudgeon and dace. In some locations anglers can catch grayling in addition to sea trout and salmon that have been reintroduced. Tactics that work are au toc - using natural baits, spinning and fly-fishing.

The département is divided into four river basins.

The Dordogne River, the Corrèze River, the Vézère River and the Vienne River basin.

Dordogne River Basin

River Chavanon: fishable between Puy de Dôme and the Corrèze. The Chavanon has its source at the confluence of the Méouzette and Ramade streams. These are tributaries of the Dordogne River that join from the right bank. The confluence with the Dordogne is at the Retenue de Bort les Orgues.

The Chavanon is a representative watercourse for this region, containing riffs and gorges in downstream areas. Stretches vary from a pastoral setting to quite wild surroundings. Easy access is available to upstream areas around Moulin de Laroche then from the RN-89: until the first old railway tunnel between Eygurande and Merlines. Following here there is very difficult access into the gorges. There is a good population of trout and a programme of re-introduction of grayling conducted in collaboration with the FD du Pay de Dôme – local angling club. All types of angling methods work well here.

Parcours de Grâciation are free catch and release river stretches that are situated upstream of l'Hospital de la Cellette.

Local angling club AAPMA de Merlines manages these river stretches.

Recommended angling stretches: fish form the source of the Chavanon following on from here to the Ruisseaux de La Meouzette and the Ramade. From the RN-89 downstream to the old railway tunnel.

Interesting affluents – the Barricade a tributary of the Chavanon and the Dognon, are nearby affluents of the Dordogne. Plan d'eau de l'Abeille (13ha) situated at Merlines has its own regulations.

www.pechemouchefrance.com offers free download videos of trout rivers e.g upper Dordogne River

Accommodation - Hotel-Restaurant: Le Chavanon at Merlines, La demi Lune at Chalon d'Aix situated 3km from Merlines. Bar-Hotel Peuf at Merlines Gare – station

Useful addresses- Pavillon des Portes de la Corrèze de Monestier Merlines Tel, 0555944032, Mairie de Merlines Tel, 0555943220.

Worth visiting on your day off - Viaduc du Chavanon de l'autoroute A89

Maps to use - IGN verte 49 IGN bleue 2432 O 2332 E and Michelin 73

Diège River: a tributary of the Dordogne River entering from its right bank at the Retenue de Maèges. It follows a course of 45 km from its source on the plateau des Mille Vaches and is similar in character to the Chavanon River.

Local angling clubs AAPPMA d'Ussel, Sornac and Bort les Orgue manage these river stretches.

Interesting riverstretches: parcours mouche no-kill situated from Ussel to downstream of the RN-89.

Interesting tributaries: Sarsonne River, right bank, confluence at Usssel, 5-6 m average channel width and quite shallow, it supports a good population of brown trout. The Liège River has the same profile its confluence is situated by St. Pardoux le Vieux. It might also be worth investigating the Dozane River.

Offices du Tourisme located at Ussel Tel, 0555721150, Sornac Tel, 0555946266, Bort les Orgues Tel, 0555960249.

Maps to use - IGN verte 49 IGN bleue 2232O, 2233O, 2333 E.

Triouzoune River is classified as 1st category except the Retenue EDF de Neuvic that is classed as 2nd category. The river's course is entirely within the département's borders. Its source is found on the plateau de Mille Vaches. And its end at the confluence with the Dorogne River is in the Retenue de l'Aigle.

It's a small river with different types of channel combining faster riffs with slower meandering pasture and some steeper rocky cascades. The setting is rural to wild especially downstream of the Retenue de Neuvic.

Access to upstream stretches is easy, downstream more difficult. There is a good trout population that responds well to all angling techniques.

The AAPPMA de Nuevic, Meymac and Ussel manage the river.

Campisite and gîtes are located around Neuvic.

Offices du Tourisme de Neuvic: Tel, 0555958878, and at Meymac: Tel, 0555951843.

Places to visit: at Neuvic, the plan d'eau, the Maison de la Pêche et de l'eau, Musée H. Queille, Meymac.

Maps to use: IGN verte 49 IGN bleue 2333 E 2333 O 2334 O.

Vianon River is a tributary entering from the right bank of the Luzège River whose confluence is at the Retenue de Sant Pantéléon de Lapleau. Located entirely in the département, it is 15 km long. Its source is on the plateau de Mille Vaches. It's a small river with various phases. Meandering through the plains upstream, downstream there are riffs. The setting is rural to wild. There is easy access and a good trout population.

Interesting river stretches: Palisse and St. Hilaire Luc

Accommodation: Campsites at Egletons, Neuvic, and Lapleau. Villages de Vacances at Egletons and Lapleau. Numerous gîtes – reservations required. Hotels in most of the towns.

Useful address: Offices du Tourisme de Neuvic Tel, 0555958878 and Lapleau Tel, 0555275883.

Maps: IGN verte 49 IGN bleue 2234 O.

Luzège River is a tribuary of the Dordogne River entering on its right bank at the Retenue du Chastong situated at Laval sur Luzège. Located entirely in the département, 30 km long. Source is on the plateau de Mille Vaches. A small river with weak current, meandering along plains, to the north of the N-89 then a torrent in the gorges until the Retenue EDF de Sant Pantéléon adjacent to to Lapleau.

From here until the confluence there isn't much water. There is a rural setting with impressive scenery in the gorges, easy access to upstream stretches but more difficult downstream. There is a good population of trout but they are sometimes fussy.

Interesting tributaries: Ruisseau d'Ambrugeat, upstream and downstream situated of plan d'eau de Séchemaille, managed by the AAPPMA de Meymac, good population of brown trout. La Soudeillette and le Deiro, small rivers classed as $1^{\text{ère}}$ category, very pure, magnificent setting, towards Egletons. Good population of wild brown trout, all techniques work well. Including au toc - bait fishing and spinning. Managed by AAPPMA de Meymac and Egletons.

Parcours de pêche: Maussac, Pont de la Violette, Pont des Bouyges, Pont du Chambon at Lapleau, Laval sur Luzège.

Useful contacts: Offices du Tourisme d'Egletons Tel, 0555930434, de Meymac: Tel, 0555951843, Lapleau Tel, 0555275883 and Neuvic Tel, 0555958878.

On your day off: Meymac: Centre d'arts Contemporains, le Mont Bessou, highest point in the Corrèze (986m a.s.l.), Egletons and its surroundings: Château de Ventadour (Moustier Ventadour), le viaduc du rocher noir, la vieille Eglise - church at St. Pantaléon de Lapleau. Plans d'eau d'Egletons and Séchemailles.

Maps to use: IGN verte 48 IGN bleue 2234^E, 2233E.

Doustre River is 1st category except for the Retenue EDF de la Valette known locally as Lac de Marcillac this is classified as 2nd category. A tributary of the Dordogne River: on its right bank. Confluence at the Retenue de Sablier situated upstream of Argentat. Its course runs entirely within the département, its source is near Egletons. A small river with low current, winding through plains interrupted by some steeper rocky cascades. Environment varies from rural to wild. Access easy upstream but becomes more problematic further downstream.

Small population of trout, gudgeon are present upstream of Marcillac. Mixed fish population downstream of the retenue. River managed by the AAPPMA d'Egletons, Marcillac, Roche Canillac and Argentat.

Useful contacts: Office de tourisme cantonal de La Roche Canillac – district level Tel, 0555292925, Office du tourisme d'Egletons Tel, 0555930434. Mairie de Marcillac la Croisille Tel, 0555278205, Office du Tourisme d'Argentat Tel, 0555281605.

Maps: IGN verte 48, IGN bleue 2235O, 2235E, 2234O, 2233O.

Maronne River: tributary of the Dordogne River by its left bank, confluence is situated downstream of Argentat. Average type of river for the region. Average current but experiences significant fluctuations in flow downstream of the Retenue EDF du Gour Noir and Hautefage. There is a good trout population along its whole course but larger specimens are caught especially around the parcours de pêche – designated fishing stretches and grayling in downstream areas where fly-fishing proves particularly effective. Access is easy. Except for downstream parcours de pêche stretches where anglers requires a more studied approach.

Parcours de pêche: La Maronne, good quality water situated by the Ruines de Merle, at St. Geniez-Ô-Merle, discharge from the Barrage du Gour Noir - dam. This river stretch is located in a deep wooded valley where the hand of man has not ventured except for the creation of the suspension bridge. For 10 km, a series of smooth runs and riffs, a good population of wild brown trout, gudgeon and dace, fly-fishing is recommended. Rigorous and sports fishing experience.

River is managed by the AAPPMA Argentat, St Privat and Sexcles.

Useful contacts: Office du Tourisme de St. Privat Tel: 0555282877.

Maps: IGN verte 48, IGN bleue 2235O.

Cère River is a tributary of the Dordogne River from its right bank, confluence is situated downstream of Beaulieu. Average type of river for the area, average flow, quite deep, often there is difficult access, wild surroundings. Good trout population, minimum size for capture is 23cm. Fly-fishing is especially rewarding on many stretches along this river.

River is managed by AAPPMA Beaulieu and Sexcles.

Maps to use: IGN verte 48, IGN bleue 2236O 2236E.

Corrèze River basin

The Corrèze is classified as 1st category from its source at the foot of the Monédières at St Yrieux du Déjalat up to its confluence with the river Vézère at the Pont de Cornil. A river course extending over 100 km. At its source the brook favours au toc - bait fishing, loads of small wild brown trout are present especially upstream of Corrèze where you will encounter a river of average width with a varied current and attractive fishing swims around Tulle. Access is usually pretty good. There is a good trout population often mixed up with a variety of other fish species. All angling techniques work well here.

Interesting tributaries and parcours de pêche: the Solanne and the Céronne, small tributaries on the right bank of the Corrèze, confluence at Tulle: it attracts many visitors.

Parcours de grâciation touristique are free to fish river stretches specially intended for visiting anglers, with periodic stocking of rainbow trout: situated downstream of Tulle. Parcours de grâciation patrimonial are free to fish river stretches without stocking found on the Saint Bonnette.

The Corrèze Riverand its tributaries are classified blue and at this sign or where you find Atlantic salmon, fishing is banned. Please return with care to the water any salmon caught accidentally.

This river is controlled by: AAPPMA St. Yrieux le Déjalat, Corrèze and Tulle.

Accommodation: campsite at St. Yrieux.

Useful contacts: Offices du Tourisme d'Egletons Tel, 0555930434, CorrèzeTel, 0555213282 and Tulle Tel, 0555265961, Mairie de St. Yrieix Tel, 0555930994.

Maps: IGN verte 48 IGN bleue 2134 E 2135 O 2233 O 2233 E 2234 O.

Montagne River is a tributary of the Corrèze entering by its left bank at Tulle. Contained entirely within the département with its source in the north west of Egletons, it runs for 30 km. At its source the brook is clam and meandering encouraging au toc, there are plenty of small wild brown trout. Thereafter the river gradually picks up steam especially downstream of Gimel where the course varies until reaching Tulle. Access is mostly easy. A good trout population is present.

River is managed by the AAPPMA Egletons, Corrèze and Tulle.

Parcours de pêche of interest: Vitrac, Eyrein, Gimel. La Bonnette, tributary left bank, confluence at Tulle, a few visitors.

Accommodation: campsites at Egletons, Corrèze and Tulle.

On your day off: visit the cascades de Gimel.

Maps to use: IGN verte 48 IGN bleue 2134 E 2233 O 2234 E.

Vimbelle River is a tributary of the Corrèze Riveron on its right bank. Confluence is upstream of Tulle. Course is entirely within the département for 15 km. A small river with little depth, varying currents over channel bed of sand and gravel. Often wooded banks, easy access. Good trout population. Best when fished spinning or au toc.

This river is managed by: AAPPMA Corrèze and Tulle.

Useful contacts: Offices du Tourisme de Corrèze Tel, 0555213282, de Tulle Tel, 0555265961.

Maps to use: IGN verte 48 IGN bleue 2133 E 2134 E.

Maumont River is formed by combination of the Maumont Noir and Maumont Blanc, a tributary of the Corrèze River on its right bank. Course is entirely within the département but it's classified as 2nd category after the confluence with the river Clan situated towards the Pont de Salomond. There are fly-fishing possibilities in the upstream parcours de pêche river stretches where mixed fish species populations are present.

River is managed by the AAPPMA Allasac, Roseau Gaillard, Tullle and Pays de Brive.

Useful contacts: Offices du Tourisme at Allassac Tel 0555849248, Brive Tel, 0555240880, Tulle Tel, 0555265961.

Maps to use: IGN verte IGN bleue.

Vézère River basin

Vézère River is classified as 1st category from its source among the heathers on the plateau des Mille Vaches at St. Merd les Ousines downstream to the SCNF viaduct Uzerche where it passes into 2nd category water.

At its source the brook is calm and sinuous, in the peat bogs then it crosses several EDF reservoirs classified as 2nd category. These are the Retenues de Viam, Treignac and Peyrissac. Between each reservoir the river channel widens, to 12 m downstream of Peyrissac. The fish population is mixed but there are plenty of brown trout. The gradient of the valley and slope of the banks vary. Access is mostly easy. Fly-fishing is recommended especially at the start of the season.

River is managed by AAPPMA Bugeat, Treignac and Uzerche.

Interesting tributaries: the Petit Vézère located around St. Merd les Ousines. La Soudaine, a small river 12 km long, joins the Vézère by its right bank, source is on the plateau Mille Vaches, and its confluence towards Affieux. A good trout population exists, spinning and au toc fishing methods work well. Le Bradascou, a small tributary entering on the right bank is 20 km long, its confluence with the Vézère is situated downstream of Uzerche. Pastoral surroundings, various stretches, a good head of trout are present.

Useful contacts: Offices du Tourisme de Bugeat Tel, 0555951868, TreignacTel, 0555981504 UzercheTel, 0555731571.

Maps to use: IGN verte 41 and 48 IGN bleue 2132 E 2133 O 2133 E 2232 O 2232 E.

Loyre River is a tributary of the Vézère River it lies entirely within the département along a 20 km course. Its source is between Lubersac and Uzerche and it passes into 2nd category by Objat at its confluence with the Rozay. It isa small river not more than 4-6 m wide with little depth: and is fed by many streams. The current is strong and varied, the banks are often wooded; access is sometimes difficult in upstream stretches. Previously it supported a lot of fish, now the middle reaches are quite troubled. There are plenty of orchards and a small trout population.

River is managed by AAPPMA Pompadour, Vigeois and Juillac.

Interesting tributaries: La Loyre, from its confluence with the Rosay up to the Moulin de Mialet and the Rozay. Plan d'Eau Fédéral de Vigeois.

Useful contacts: district tourist office Tel, 0555259673,Vigeois Tel, 0555989644, Juillac Tel, 0555256996.

Maps to use: IGN verte 48 IGN bleue 2033 E, 2034 E, 2133 O, 2134 O.

Logne River is a tributary of the Vézère Riveris and lies entirely within the département along a 15 km course. Its source is towards Puy d'Yssandon and its confluence with the Vézère is at Rivière de Mansac. There is a mixture of coarse and game fish.

Managed by AAPPMA Roseau Gaillard.

Maps to use: IGN verte IGN bleue.

Vienne River basin

Vienne River is 1st category from its source in Corrèze département until its entrance into Creuse département where it passes into 2nd category. Water. From the Ruisseau du plateau de Mille Vaches, it gradually widens until it reaches 5 m across it supports a high density of beautiful trout. The river course is varied and it offers easy access.

River managed by AAPPMA Peyrelevade-Tarnac-Toy-Viam.

Interesting tributaries: a number of small affluents are located around Peyrelevade. On the Chandouille affluent is the Retenue EDF de Chammet this reservoir is classed as 2nd category water.

Accommodation: campsites at Peyrelevade and Tarnac.

Useful contacts: Mairies de Peyrelevade – town hall Tel, 0555947312, Tarnac Tel, 0555955301, Toy-Viam Tel, 0555954410.

Maps to use: IGN verte 41 IGN bleue 2131 O 2131 E 2232 O 2232 E.

Auvézère River is a tributary on the right bank of the Isle River its course runs in the département up to Ségur le Château. A good population of trout is found in upstream reaches.

There are numerous écluses - locks on the parcours de pêche – fishing stretches, creating small retenues - reservoirs one of which supports a population of poisson blanc – general coarse fish species and some perch and pike.

Useful contacts: Mairie de Lubersac – town hall Tel, 0555735014.

Maps to use: IGN verte IGN bleue

Parcours de Grâciation – free fishing, catch and release stretches, denoted by a star on the regional map at the start of this chapter.

Three colour codes indicate these fishing reserves they are yellow, blue and green. Yellow fishing reserves represent the basic model of catch and release areas. Blue reserves are based on the idea of the first parcours de pêche established on the Corrèze River by the Iles at Tulle opened in 2003. This particular reserve's achievement was in attracting 300 anglers within 3 months by holding free fishing competitions. The distinction from the first type of reserve is that this stretch stocks rainbow trout.

The blue reserves have been established in population centres with economic activity. Centred mainly around Brive and to the north of this city. On 1 km stretches that had previously experienced degradation: and where access is now made easy. In 2006 a further 9 fishing reserves were created. They are well signposted and easy to find. There are 8 fish releases planned at a rate of 15-30 kg per fishing resrve.

Dates of trout releases: weekend of 25, 26 March, weekend of Rameaux – Palm Sunday, Pâques - Easter, May 1st, May 8th, feast of Ascension, which coincides with weekend at the river bank, except fête de la Pêche – angling festival, weekend of Pentecôte and finally 14th July. Depending on river levels, in times of distress when stockings may be transferred to alternative rivers or delayed.

The blue fishing reserves are listed here

Bassin Basse Vézère/Auvézère
AAPPMA de Lubersac
Parcours du Pont Lagorce (1 km stretch) river Auvézère
Upstream border: Moulin de la Douverie
Downstream border: Pont de Lagorce

Bassin Basse Vézère/Auvézère
AAPPMA de Pompadour
Parcours du Moulin de la Jante (750 m stretch) river Auvézère
Upstream border: Moulin de la Jante
Downstream border: Pont du Theil

Bassin Basse Vézère/Auvézère
AAPPMA de Juillac
Parcours des deux Moulins 800 m stretch of river Auvézère
Upstream border: Moulin de Poudou
Downstream border: Moulin Bleu

Bassin Basse Vézère/Auvézère
AAPPMA d'Allassac
Parcours de Garavet (500 m stretch) river Vézère
Upstream border: 500 m upstream of the bridge
Downstream border: Pont de Garavet

Bassin Basse Vézère/Auvézère
AAPPMA de Voutezac
Parcours de Murat (1.3 km stretch) river Loyre

Upstream border: Digue du canal de Murat - lock
Downstream border : confluence of the Loyre/canal

Bassin Basse Vézère/Auvézère
AAPPMA du Roseau Gaillard
Parcours de Grand Roche (1 km stretch) river Maumont
Upstream border: confluence with the Saulières
Downstream border: 300 m upstream of the A20 road

Bassin Basse Vézère/Auvézère
AAPPMA d'Objat
Parcours des grands Prés (850 m stretch) river Loyre
Upstream border: 150 m downstream of the passe à poisons – fish pass
Downstream border: déversoir du Plan d'eau – overflow channel from lake

Bassin Basse Vézère/Auvézère
AAPPMA du Roseau Gaillard
Parcours des Cascades (500 m stretch) river Sorpt
Upstream border: Pont de Roziers
Downstream border: 150 m upstream of the pont du Soulier

Bassin Corrèze
AAPPMA des Pêcheurs du Pays de BriveLubersac
Parcours de Claredent (1.2 km) stretch river Corrèze
Upstream border: Pont de Claredent
Downstream border: Pont de Jayles to 150 m downstream of the pont du Soulier

The green fishing reserves provide a sanctuary for native wild brown trout and therefore receive no fish stockings. These fishing reserves are located in streams in upstream areas of river basins. These types of reserves are open for free fishing under certain conditions in order to monitor fish stocks. For more details on how fishing reserves are classified get in touch with the local angling federation.

Use barbless hooks only. Use of artificial lures is allowed for instance fly, spinning and minnow lures, but the use of natural baits is banned, with the exception of parcours de pêche on the Corrèze and Deiro Rivers where all angling techniques are allowed.

Trout and grayling must be returned in a sympathetic manner to the water. The Carte de Pêche – angling licence specific to the water is free is obtainable from the local AAPPMA although anglers are limited by number each day.

The following list contains all three types of free to fish, catch and release fishing reserves.

Dordogne River situated between the old d'Argentat bridge and a line located 50 m upstream of the confluence with the Souvigne River.

Dordogne River situated between the passerelle des Aubarèdes – footbridge. Upstream: to 50 m upstream of the pont de la départementale 940 - road, all of the channel known as Gabariers that's included in these fishing reserves, situated at Altillac and Beaulieu.

Vézère River between the station d'épuration de Treignac – water purifier plant and the old pont de Treignac. Vézère River between the ruisseau du Mazeaud, upstream and to the right of the borne km n°1 – km marker located on the D97 road, situated downstream at Bugeat.

Petite Vézère River is situated between the carrières de Pérols – quarry, upstream and the pont de l'ancienne usine hydroélectrique du Moulin de Barthou downstream, in the vicinity of Bugeat and Pérols. Maronne River, fishing reserve is situated 200 m downstream of the ruisseau de la prade and 300 m upstream of the pont de la RD 13- border of towns of ST Geniez Ô Merles and Goulles.

Corrèze River, fishing between the two ponts routiers de franchissement de la RN 89- road bridges situated either side of the tunnel known as des Iles, by Chameyrat and Cornil.

Saint Bonnette River, fishing between the pont de St Mur and the pont de Palissou, at Espagnac.

Deiro River, fishing at Egletons for 1 km upstream from the confluence with Soudeillette.

Doustre River, fishing at Saint Bazile de la Roche between the pont sur la V.C. called la rivière downstream and la prise d'eau du bief du Moulin du Château – water intake channel, upstream. Chavanon River, this fishing reserve is called a parcours interdépartemental Corrèze/Puy de Dôme – fishing reserves bordering two départements, situated upstream of l'Hopital de la Céllette – good fishing for grayling.

New for 2006 season

The plan d'eau du Château de Sédières is open from the second Saturday in May.

2nd category waters managed by the départemental angling federation have a 3-rod limit.

There is a Lovely lake covering 20 ha at the foot of Château, it has excellent access, good parking and a path round lake. This is a family destination; there is a kiddies play area and frequent art exhibitions.

http://www.pechetruite.com/Lacs_reservoirs/correze.htm
Weekend trout fishing – accommodation near réservoir de la Demi-Lune

LOZÈRE 48

Angling information contact:	Fédération de Pêche Lozère 12, Avenue Paulin Daudé - 48000 Mende. Tel, 04 66 65 36 11 Fax: 04 66 65 92 37 Email: infos@peche48.com
General information:	Comité Départemental du Tourisme 14, bd henri-Bourrillon BP 4 – 48001 Mende cedex Tel, 33 (0) 4 66656000 Fax, 33 (0) 4 66650355 Email: cdt@lozere-tourisme.com www.lozere-tourisme.com

Mende tourist board: www.ot-mende.fr/flyfishing
British partnership - ClubFishFrance: www.clubfishfrance.com

Lozère is situated in southwest France bordering the Central Massif, just one hour's drive along the motorway south of Clermont Ferrand. To the east is the Ardèche. To the west: Aveyron and to the south Hérault.

For the angler Lozère is made up of four main areas. The vast Aubrac plateau, the tight Cevennes valleys in the south east, the wooded mountains of Margeride in the north east and flowing westwards the Grand Causes of the rivers Tarn and Jonte, great fishing is available everywhere. The rivers Lot, Altier, Tarn, Truyère, Bès and Jonte contain 2,700 kilometres of superb 1st category rivers stuffed full of trout.

Local anglers have a way of preserving their regions unique character. In expressing a deep attachment to their land and rivers, they decided to operate a policy of non-reciprocity with angling organisations from neighbouring départements. They are the only département to have broken away from the national fishing federation.

Variety is the key. Most of the rivers originate in the Central Massif, seeping through limestone, basalt, granite and shale to create rivers with distinct characters. The Lozère is an ideal fishing destination for fishermen from all over France and beyond.

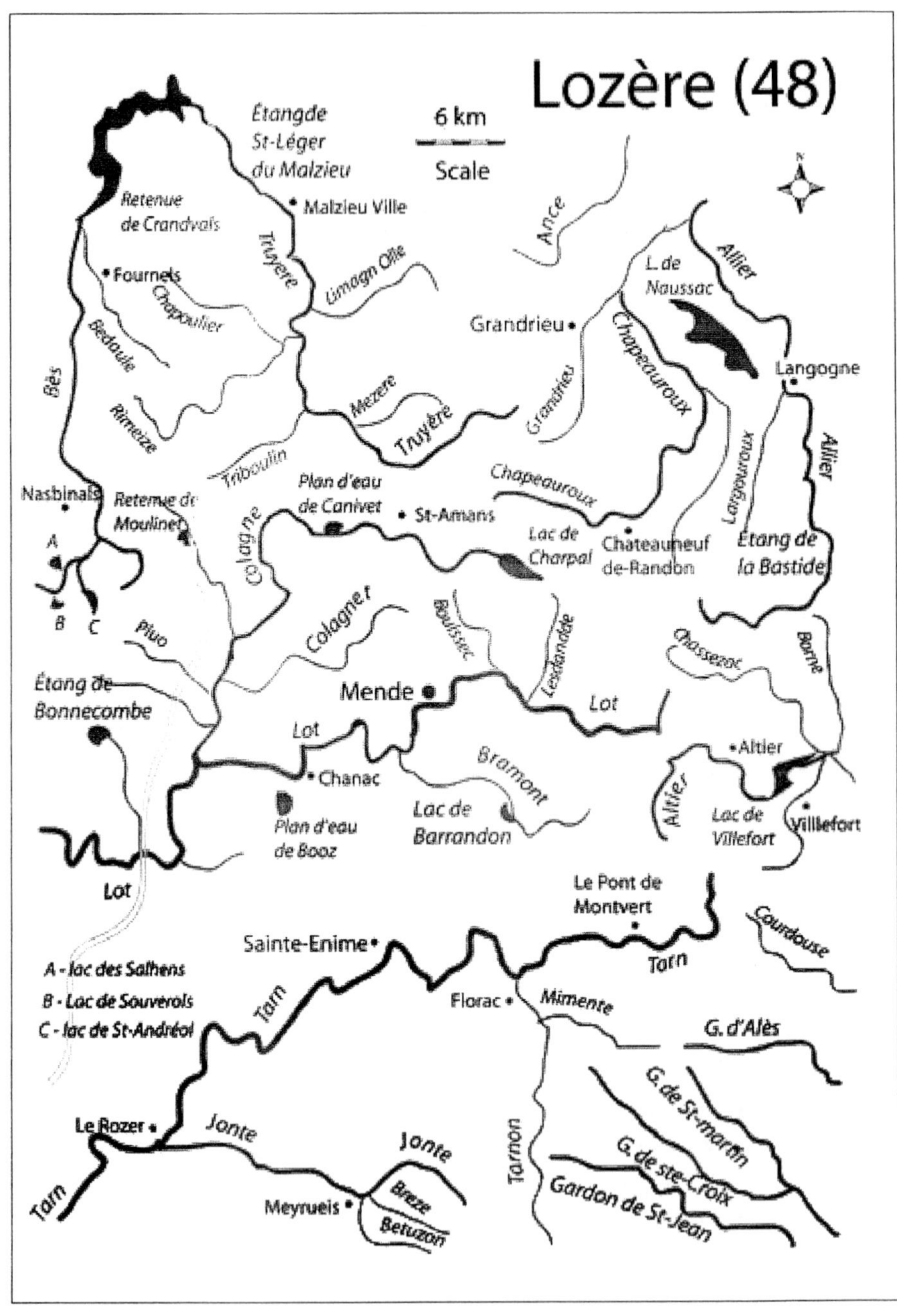

It's also a place of note for professional angling guides who work closely with the tourism office in this département to develop the region's huge potential. Gathered within an organisation that controls five angling guide services spread throughout Lozère, their goal is to attract fly-fishermen to their great rivers and lakes. Details are given below.

An innovation in the 2005 angling season was the introduction of young rainbow trout in superb condition with the aim of attracting sporting anglers to river stretches classified as zones de piedmont situated on the Tarn River from Quézac to Prades and the Lot River downstream of Chanac, where existing roach, rudd and bream occupy 95% of the ecological niche.

The rainbow trout it is hoped will prosper in the wild in order to grow to large sizes in thede rivesr. Wild brown trout at present occupy 99% of the Lozérien river basin. These two species of trout can easily live side by side in the larger rivers.

In the deepest of gorges in the heart of the canyons eroded by water over millennia the angler cannot help but be impressed by the elevated rocky silhouette. This is a spiritual place.

The Guide de Pêche free fishing guide booklet is available from: Comité Departemental du Tourisme de la Lozère, 14 Boulevard Henri-Bourrillon 48001 Mende Cedex Tel, 0466656000 Fax, 0466492796.

Licences: anglers in general must be in procession of the La Carte de Pêche Complète to fish the rivers and lakes in Lozère the great majority are classified as 1st category waters. The annual angling licence costs €65 and is valid for one year.

The Carte de Pêche Complète is made up from the Taxe Piscicole - a stamp in your Carte de Pêche booklet that proves that you have paid the French fishing licence tax for one département, and the Cotisation Statutaire - statutory contribution in order to fish in Lozère.

Pensioners and anglers under 16 years old by the 1st January are exempt from paying the Taxe Piscicole provided they fish with a single rod equipped with two hooks at most but are not permitted to spin just fly-fish. So they are left to pay €15.

The Carte de Pêche Vacances can be purchased in summer between 1st June and 18th September that allows fishing for 15 consecutive days except on Lac de Nasseau where the fishing holiday period runs from 1st June through 30th September. It costs €36.

Anglers under 16 years of age before 1st January qualify for a Carte de Pêche Jeune. This permits the young angler to fish on all the rivers and lakes using any mode of fishing. It costs €25.

Carte de Pêche Journalière is a day ticket available for fishing the following lakes in Lozére: Naussac, Bayard-Villefort, Rachas, Puylaurent, Roujanel, Pied de Borne, Ganivet, Moulinet, Booz, Andéol, Born, Souveyrols and Salhens. It costs €15.

The angling licence is free for anglers less than twelve years old on the 1st January who may fish with one rod and a maximum of 2 hooks. Even though it's free children must be in procession of the Carte Exonérée.

Because Lozère has no reciprocal arrangements with other départements in France then if you have purchased your angling licence in another département you will be required to pay the cotisation statutaire that is calculated as the price of the Carte de Pêche less the price of the Taxe Piscicole.

Cotisation statutaire: Carte Annuelle - €37. Carte Jeune - €15. Carte Vacances €23. Carte Journalière - €12.

Lozère département is not affiliated with the Entent Haliautique et Grand Ouest. And therefore has no reciprocal arrangements with other départements in France. Conversely a Carte de Pêche purchased in Lozère will be due for payment of the Taxe Piscicole again in another département.

To order a fishing licence in advance of your trip send a cheque made payable to Fédération de Pêche de Lozère at: Fédération de Pêche de Lozère 12 Avenue Paulin Daudé, 48000 Mende, France. Include details of your birth; your name, your address, and passport number written on back of passport size photo.

A video called Pêche à la Mouche en Lozère – Fly-fishing in Lozère is available from the Fédération de Pêche de Lozère, send a cheque to their address above for €17 including postage. Or email them for more information.

A map of the river basins is also available please ask for the Carte des cours d'eau de Lozère (70 by 50cm). Cost is €12 including postage.

www.lozerepechemouche.com
this website that gives good pictures and introductions to this region's rivers and local fly lure patterns

Season times

Except for the rivière Bès situated downstream of the restitution de la centrale du Vergne (power station).

Trout- 12th March through 18th September.
Common grayling- 14th May through 31st December.
Pike – close season from 30th January through 14th May.
Zander – close season from 1st May through 11th June.

The retenue de Grandvals lake is managed by the neighbouring Département du Cantal.

Rules and Regulations

In general anglers can only fish with one rod, a maximum of two hooks or three fly lures.

No ground baiting or use of maggots is allowed. No live baiting is allowed on all first category rivers and lakes except for lacs de Nausea, Salhens, Souveyrols, Born and Saint-Andéol.

Dead baiting and spinning is banned from the second Saturday in March through to the third Friday in April on all 1st category waters except for lacs de Naussac, Salhens, Souveyrols, Born, and Saint-Andéol.

No wading in the river Jonte is allowed from its source until the ravine de Castèle from the second Saturday in March through to the third Friday in April.

To protect spawning grounds wading is banned from the second Saturday in March through to the third Friday in May on the Allier River downstream of the Pont de Rogleton by the town of Luc. And in the Chapeauroux River downstream of the Pont du Rodier in vicinity of the town of Châteauneuf de Randon.

The Association Agréée pour la Pêche et la Protection du Milieu Aquatique de Pont de Monvert (AAPPMA de la Haute Vallée du Tarn) have their own regulations, for details see below.

Étangs Touristiques de Pêche – tourist fishing lakes

The étangs de Barrandon, La Bastide, and Saint-Léger du Malzieu are open for fishing from 1st July through to the third Sunday in September. From 9 a.m. till noon then again from 2p.m. through to 7p.m. From 30th April through to 30th June these lakes except for étang de Barrandon, are open for the same hours at weekends and public holidays. Étang de Barrandon is open for the same hours all week from 14th May through 30th June. Tariff is €10.5 for 5 trout, €19 for ten trout and €2 for one fish.

Minimum size of trout is between 23 and 25cm depending on location. Please consult the free Guide de Pêche booklet available locally for details. Minimum size for common grayling is 30cm. Pike, 50cm and zander 40cm (on the second category barrage de Grandvals)

Bag limit is 10 fish including a maximum of 5 common grayling. On waters where the minimum size for trout is 25cm there is a 5-bag limit. On the lakes there is an 8-bag limit.

The **Tarn River** has its source roughly 1500 m above sea level on the southern col of Mont-Lozère, known as the home of the Ordre des Templiers. It flows through 80 km of the Lozérien département evolving through different stages but essentially it's a river of gorges.

First cutting through granite rock, after Pont de Montvert the river flows past the slopes of the montagne du Bougès to the south and finally the slopes of the Mont-Lozère to the north. To the bottom of the drop where it's joined by the river Tarnet here it has slowly eroded the bedrock to form the famous gorges that bear the river's name. It's at the village of Rozier where the two gorges peter out that the Tarn River exits the département.

Many consider the Tarn at the point beside the Chateau La Caze to be one of the most beautiful rivers in Europe. Upstream in the faster currents the trout are more taciturn. Further downstream the trout become less impetuous and grow larger in the slower flow feeding heavily on the fauna and benefiting from the calcium rich water.

As well as smaller fish such as minnows and gudgeon there are very large barbeaux fluviatiles – river barbel present, dace and chub that swim upstream as far as Vernède. All these fish species will take a fly lure. The Tarn River is classified as 1st category along its whole course in the Lozère département.

Réserves de Pêche: 300 m stretch of the Tarn River at Bedoues: fish from the Barrage de la Vernêde to 300 m downstream. And a 220 m stretch of the Tarn River at Le Pont de Montvert, fish from the sortie de la Microcentral – exit of mini-power station downstream to the abattoir de Pont de Montvert.

Parcours amont - upstream fishing stretches

In the shadow of the summit of Mont-Lozère the Tarn River resembles a lively brook then it meanders through a wetland plain punctuated by granite rock outcrops until a change in gradient. Now begin the first set of gorges between Pont-du-Tarn and Villeneuve.

On this stretch there are plenty of small trout. With the exception of the upstream section which is only suitable for fishing au toc – bait method the rest of the course encourages the use of very light spinners and fly-fishing.

Middle reaches

The first change occurs in the Tarn's course upstream of Villeneuve where the river is engulfed in a granite gorge with a very steep drop that descends in a succession of spectacular rapids through deep gorges after which it is joined by a tributary the Alignon River a little upstream of Pont-de-Montvert.

Fly-fishing or au toc method on this difficult to reach stretch requires anglers to be in good physical shape because the terrain is broken.

Second section: after the confluence with the Alignon River that adds to the flow the Tarn River crosses Pont-de-Montvert. Here the granite bedrock appears once again in a narrow and untamed valley covered in chestnut trees.

The valley ends around Cocurès a little before its junction with the Tarnon River at Florac. Forming successive pools in fast water the channel here encourages all manner of methods for trout fishing. Natural larvae become increasingly populous as the Tarn River matures.

Downstream reaches

This section starts at theconfluence with an important tributary theTarnon a beautiful river with its source in vicinity of Aigoual. The Tarn grows even bigger downstream from Mimente and immediately upstream of Florac the Tarn becomes a beautiful river.

Already a powerful force the Tarn carves through limestone gorges where hundreds of kayak canoes take tourists gliding through the clear water in July and August. In these gorges the riverbed is sometimes made from limestone flagstones that have been stacked up by the current or eroded smooth and punctuated by volcanic boulders where the trout hang out.

Dry fly nymph fishing proves very popular here in the gorges with local anglers. And the deep pools hold large trout that only a minnow imitation lure can entice.

The Mimente River flows 26 km through gorges that run parallel with the route de la Barre des Cévennes, joining the Tarnon then the Tarn at Florac. Take the NR 106 towards Cassagnas. Just downstream towards Crozes there is parking. Further downstream at St Julien d' Arpaon the river gets calmer and is a good place to start fishing.

Angling licences: Mme Boiral Tel 0466450317, M. Canonge Tel 04 66450442, M. Nicolas Tel 04451281.

The Tarnon River is especially scenic around the villages of Vebron and Vanels. From Florac take the D 907 road. At Vebron cross over the small bridge and follow the route along the river: descending along its right bank. After 500 m take the left fork for the river.

Trees that prevent fishing from the top of the bank. Cast at the end of runs where the trout often hold up. Select grey emerger fly lures. In deeper pools chub reaching a kilo can be caught. A stonewall creates an interesting swim in the middle of the stretch. Non-slip waders are useful in this slippery zone.

Angling licences: Tabac, L'Esplanade, Florac 48400 Tel, 0466452763. Boiral, Quincaillerie, 54 av. Jean Monestier, Florac 48400 Tel, 0466450317. Tabac de la Source, Place de la Mairie, Florac 48400 Tel, 0466450452.

The Tarn Gorges

From June to December an endless flotilla of boats cruise this river. It's advisable then that anglers fish the river in early morning or later on or visit from spring through middle of June.

The upstream stretch towards Pont de Monvert has narrow granite gorges with the river flowing through tight passageways far below. Downstream a little ways before reaching Enime – Florac, fishing is good at Castelbouc.

Take the From Florac NR 106 until Espagnac. Now head for Enimie via Quézac by taking the D07B. At the exit to the viewpoint a small winding road descends to Castebouc. The stretch contains fast runs interrupted by a series of deep holes. Evenings promise good results when adopting nymph-fishing methods. Both dry and sunken line work well. At Mallène downstream there are a fewer number of bigger and more warier trout. In this instance try bait fishing.

Angling licences: Boulangerie Nadal, La Malène 48210 Tel, 0466485127. Barbut Claude- Bimbeloterie, Rue de la Combe- Ste

Enimie 48210 Tel, 0466485658. Coups de Coeur, Auberge des Laubies Anne-Marie Romain, Les Laubies 48000 St-Etienne-du-Valdonnez Tel, 0466480125.

Accommodation: Gite 3 Epis de Quezac, Rémi et Françoise Mâcon 43, rue Notre Dame 48 320 Quézac Tel, + 33 (0) 466442299 Mobile: + 33 (0) 6 98 18 80 21 Email: famire@aol.com

Bès River – Aubrac plateau

This is the most recognised river on the plateau de l'Aubrac, beginning at 1400 m a.s.l. the water runs brown due to the existence of peat bogs as it flows through green fields covered in flowers then plummeting into a deep canon. Disappearing into the large retenue de Grandvals - lake: then joining the Truyère river.

The Bès river is classified as 1st category except for a 400 m stretch downstream from the centrale hydroélectrique du Vergne - powerstation to a point level with its opening in the retenue de Grandvals. This is the only section of river classed as 2nd category in the Lozère département.

The Bès River supports a healthy head of hard fighting brown trout they display a dark livery. Many that are caught in middle and downstream stretches reach 30 cm in length. Every season beautiful specimens exceeding 1 kg are caught by anglers using decoy minnow type lures or dry fly. At this higher altitude the fly hatchings take place later than usual commencing late June. All along the river young anglers can catch tons of minnows and gudgeon. And for the expert angler there are plenty of large pike lurking in slack water and deeper parts of the river, they arrive from some lakes at Aubrac that are connected to the Bès River.

Réserves de Pêche: 800 m stretch of Bès River at Nasbinals-Marchastel, fish from the limite parcelle de M. Rossignol (p.302) – sign posted landed property downstream to the Pont de Fer – railway bridge. A second 500 m stretch of the Bès River at Nasbinals Recoules d'Aubrac: fish from the confluence with the ruisseau de Nasbinals downstream to the passerelle d'Escudières.

Upstream reaches

From the sign at Mailhebiau where the river is born at 1440 m above sea level downstream to a few hundred metres upstream of the RD 900 road that joins Nasbinals to Marvejols the Bès is a brook with a channel course that alternates between a mini torrent and racing through granite boulders and calm meanders along tree lined banks. Best angling techniques here include au toc, worms and insects on a hook.

Middle reaches

Fish from: the RD 900 road downstream to the village of Chaldette (spa facilities are present). The channel occupies a broader profile and encourages spinning with artificial lures including spoons and Rapalas, also try minnow lures and fly-fishing techniques.

At this stage the river becomes quite beautiful with a peaceful nature favouring fly-fishing but not nymph techniques because the water is cloudy. The best times to fish are when the mayfly hatchings occur and the spring floods that favour wet fly.

Downstream reaches

Upstream of the thermal springs at Chaldette there is a 3 km fly-only fishing stretch that supports hard fighting wild brown trout.

From the village of Chaldette until the opening into the retenue de Grandvals the river carves through granite gorges adopting a more torrential character. Downstream in the section from the village of Saint-Juéry until the centrale du Vergne - power station the flow is regulated, access to the shoreline is made more difficult compounded by the increase in number of gorges. Attempting to fish some swims here can prove dangerous and is not worth the risk involved.

Techniques are similar to those practised in the middle reaches. But spinning with a minnow lure is effective in the deeper pools. Remember to wear non-slip waders in the channel because the basalt rock forming parts of the riverbed is very slippery.

Colagne River

A river with dark water that enjoys a particular reputation amongst fly-anglers due to the large amount of mayflies that hatch towards the end of June that entice all the greedy trout.

Straight after its birth at 1400 m above sea level on the Plateau du Roy the river enters the Lac de Charpal that provides water for the town of Mende.

Therefore the flow out of this lake is quite lazy in nature and even more noticeable in its calmness when leaving the retenue du Ganivet on the middle stretch where it diverts towards Truyère.

Only where the river flows through the gorges upstream of Saint-Léger-de-Peyre then joined by the Crueize and Coulagnet Rivers that the Colagne River regains some vigour and flows downstream into the Lot River towards a place called Les Ajustons at the crossroads of the N 9 and N 88.

Classified as 1st category water the Colagne River supports trout, gudgeon, minnows and chub on the downstream reaches Some pike and perch are present coming from Lac de Charpal downstream of the dam and larger numbers are present upstream a little way before its source.

Réserves de Pêche: 1500 m stretch of the Coulagnet River at Montrodat-Marvejols, fish from the digue de Mr Rousset – dyke downstream to the Pont Talansier.

Upstream reaches

From its source until the Charpal the river flows through green land. The trout caught here are on the small side but are often caught using au toc method or smaller spinners and rapalas in the deeper pools nearer to the lake for catching pike and perch. These are considered vermin because the water is classified 1st category.

After the barrage and until the village of Rieutord-de-Randon the flow becomes quicker due to an increase in gradient. Employ au toc bait method or use natural insect baits casting amongst the wooded banks.

Middle reaches

1. From Rieutord-de-Randon down to the entrance to the gorges around Recoules-de-Fumas the Colagne River has a sandy bed that meanders through pasture. Trees planted by the bank and dense vegetation offer considerable cover for dry fly anglers. The best trout often hang up in the most difficult swims.

2. From Recoules-de-Fumas until just upstream of Marvejols the river flows through narrow gorges. Not many anglers visit because of the difficult terrain. There are loads of smaller trout present that are caught using a wide range of fishing methods.

Downstream stretch

From Marvejols to its confluence with the Lot River this stretch is situated in the vicinity of Ajustons. Here the river is mature in its course with a sand and pebble riverbed. Some very fine trout are present. Especially in the parcours mouche san tuer – catch and release stretches and immediately downstream of Marvejols.

There are 3 tributaries that require our attention

Tartaronne River is a brook flowing through pasture that enters the Colagne River a little after Rieutort.

Crueize River that after flowing through the well named Vallée de l'Enfer – valley of hell joins the Colagne River at Saint-Léger-de-Peyre.

Coulagnet River is also a small river flowing through gorges that joins the Colagne River at Marvejols.

Allier River - Margeride

A good way to explore this river is to take the train at Chasseradès quite near the river's source thatruns along the valley downstream to the exit of the grandes gorges du Val d'Allier. The passenger is guaranteed a great view of the wild country and a great trip.

At roughly 1410 m above sea level near Moure-de-la-Gardille the river Allier flows towards the north for 50 km before leaving the département of Lozere it is classified as 1st category water.

Lovely clear water supports trout with a beautiful speckled livery that changes during spawning to steel blue when they attain sizes in excess of 50cm. In addition to a population of ombres communs - grayling and Atlantic salmon who have thrived since the demolition of the barrage de St Etienne du Vigan. They can reach spawning grounds as far upstream as Luc.

During spawning large male common grayling can exceed 50cm in length and display a grey livery that shines like blue steel, these colour types are found nowhere else.

In this cold lively water hard fighting trout reach a modest 28-30cm in length, in the gorges. Other fish species present are gudgeon, minnows, chabot - bullhead and large barbel that mingle with trout in the shade as well as chub and dace further downstream.

Réserves de Pêche: 800 m stretch of the Allier River at Chasserades: fish from the Pont de Chabalieret downstream to the Pont du Serres.

Upstream reaches

From its source the brook descends quickly through a forest of beach trees by that time it's already a small river before crossing Bastide-Puylaurent (country manor). The trout here are small and agile. Au toc is best practised at this location although dry fly-fishing using light tackle is an option worth considering.

Middle reaches

From Bastide-Puylaurent: the river broadens and the valley widens until Langogne situated 20 km downstream. Clear water flows through alternating calm and faster stretches over granite bedrock and occasional basaltic rock where the river Allier first ran its course through originally active volcanic areas.

From Bastide-Puylaurent every trout fishing technique can be used. The wide, open riverbanks permit novice fly-anglers to get started here. And with a little practise might attempt to catch the common grayling that are present starting from the hamlet of Rogleton situated downstream of the Bastide.

Downstream reaches

A short distance after Langogne is located the barrage de Naussac II a little upstream of the confluence with the river Donozauthat contains the Barrage de Naussac I. At this point start wild canyons. And where the river becomes enclosed the current becomes a torrent. Fishing here is an adventure. Be careful. The middle stretch is fishable for trout and common grayling. The calm water encourages fly-fishing for the large common grayling, selecting wet or dry nymphs. Larger trout are caught using minnow as bait in the deeper pools that are found along the course of the river in this area.

Two tributaries of the river Allier warrant a mention

The Langouyrou River has crystal clear water descending through the forêt de Mercoire that joins the Allier River at Langogne and the Ance a small river typical of the Margeride area that joins the Allier River in the middle of the large gorges.

Les Gardons Cévenols - Cevennes

By summer the strong current of March will have all but disappeared underground, in effect the Gardons Cévenols presents a very Mediterranean character.

However this should not detract from the great fishing on offer far from built up areas. Three tributaries make up the main channel; they begin their life 700-900 m above sea level. Located in the centre of a crescent that runs from Can-de-l'Hospital in the west to the mountain slopes near Bougès in the east.

In the Vallée Longue that runs parallel to the Vallée Française along a connecting pass from Jalcreste to Saint-Julien-des-Point the water comes from the Gardon d'Alès. The Schiste covered with heather under tall chestnut trees is very popular with anglers wishing to catch wild mountain trout.

Only the area that gives rise to the Gardon de Sainte-Croix has a kartistic terrain that encourages quicker growth in the brown trout, many fish on Gardons Cévenols except for the upstream stretches that have steep gradients. Here trout reproduction is very low and also the lower reaches where coarse fish species predominate.

The Gardons Cévenols are all classified as 1st category water in département of Lozère and offer good quality fishing in clean clear water.

Réserves de Pêche: 1050 m stretch of the Gardons River at Ste. Croix V.F. – Moissac V.F. Fishing is good from the confluence with the ruisseau de Galteyrès downstream to the confluence with the ruisseau du Boujal.

Upstream reaches

Gardon de Sainte-Croix, fish from the hamlet of Gardon de Sainte-Croix until Sainte-Croix-Vallée-Française.

Gardon de Saint-Germain, fish all the stretches upstream of the hamlet of Bastides as well as the area around Gardon de St Martin.

Gardon d'Alès, fish from St Privat de Vallongue to the junction of the RN 106 and the road heading to St Hilaire de Lavit. On the upper stretches generally sporting angling but with difficult access often wooded and overgrown the Gardons run out into a series of basins and channels on a layer of schistose rock.

Here there are minnows and chub but more importantly beautiful brown trout that are caught au toc, worm or extra light fly tackle.

Downstream reaches

Gardon de Sainte-Croix puis de Mialet, fish from Sainte-Croix-Vallée-Française to the village of Bories at the border of the département.

Gardon de Saint-Germain, fish from the bastides - country houses until the confluence with the Gardon de Sainte-Croix.

Gardon d'Alès, fish from the crossroads of the RN 106 and the road to Saint-Hillaire-de Lavi until Saint-Julien-des-Points at the border of the département.

Getting gradually bigger boosted in flow by the contribution of its tributaries the Gardons reach to the bottom of the cévenoles valleys at the same time as the gradient decreases. The limpid water runs out over gravel channel beds that are continually altered in shape by successive floods.

Some deep basins are still present during the dry summers where fish find shelter. On these lower stretches the density of trout decreases at the expense of Barbeaux méridionaux – Mediterranean barbel, chub and dace. Any angling technique used in these gorges is effective. Many anglers using a buldo – bubble float with dropper flies catch lots of blageons - minnows wallowing in the current.

Around Biasses on the upper stretches of Gardon de Sainte-Croix angling is restricted to members of the local angling club. And visiting anglers please note that the rivers run dry in summer downstream of Saint-Germain-de-Calberte and from Martinet.

Truyère River - Margeride

Without doubt the Truyèr River, classed as 1st category is an angling location with a reputation that extends far beyond its borders and is most symbolic of the waters of the Margeride. Meandering majestically through fields of daffodils and woodland pines littered with granite stone villages.

Its rises in clear water at 1450 m above sea level in the Croix-de-Bor forest where the transparent water highlights the channel bed made up of granite sand and gravel. The water gets darker having passed through peat bogs especially downstream of its junction with the RN 106 road. The acidic nature of the water has evolved a distinct brown trout sub species with a unique livery part of which is a bright yellow that camouflages the fish well against the sandy river bottom.

Wild brown trout share their habitat first with minnows and dace then further downstream with chub. Downstream of Malzieu and more so in the gorges populations of pike and perch thrive that originated from the retenue de Grandvals that the Truyèr River feeds.

Réserves de Pêche: 350 m stretch of the Truyère River at Serverette, fish from the Passerelle, parcelle 107 – footbridge downstream to the levée du Béal Moulin de Blaise. 1 km stretch of the Mézère River: at St Dennis en Margeride. Fish from: the confluence with the ruisseau de l'Aldonès downstream to the pont sur RD 5.

Upstream reaches

Fish from the end of the Forêt de Bor beneath the Col des Trois Soeurs until the river's confluence with its first important tributary the Mézere in the village of Serverette. At this point the brook becomes a river. Fly tackle using a dry line is recommended but do not dismiss au toc or worms.

Middle reaches

Fish from the river's confluence with its tributary the Rimeize descending from Aubrac the Truyèr River accentuates its meanders and gets wider reaching 10 m in width. Exceptional fly-fishing is possible here from mid April. But anglers will also achieve good results using rapalas, spoons and imitation minnow lures.

Downstream reaches

Fish along stretches: between the Rimeize River. And the end of the département: a little way upstream of its entrance into the retenue de Grandvals. Ravines box in the channel a little. Thereafter the river picks up momentum as it flows through gorges straight after the town of Saint-Léger-du-Malzieu. Techniques that work very well here include au toc, and wet fly-fishing. Minnow and rapala lures when handled well often result in the capture of specimen, trout, pike and perch: in the gorges downstream from Saint-Léger-du-Malzieu.

Lastly it's worth mentioning some of the good fishing sport found in the tributaries of the Truyèr River in particular the Mézère, Triboulin, and

Limagnole Rivers but especially the wonderful Rimeize River, a tributary of the Aubrac River.

Chapeauroux River

Like the larger Allier River into which it flows at Chapeauroux on the border of the département the Chapeauroux is one of those rare French rivers to shelter three distinct salmonoid fish species. They are the Atlantic salmon, the trout and the grayling.

The salmon, king of fishes ascends this river after leaving the Atlantic Ocean 800 km behind. The river rises at 1480 m above sea level beneath the signal de Randon soon after the Chapeauroux becomes a more sedate river. Meandering through wetlands, pasture and peat bogs by which its waters acquire a reddish brown hue and increased acidity. This acidity combined with a relative deficiency in fish food supply restricts the size of trout but does confer onto them a special livery.

This is a small river rarely reaching 10 m in width and is classified as 1st category water along its whole course. Its banks are surrounded by green flora and in the spring a riot of flowers never fails to raise a smile.

Réserves de Pêche: 850 m stretch of the Chapeauroux River situated at St Bonnet de Montauroux, fish from parcelle 867 – signposted on the ground downstream to the Pont de St Bonnet de Montauroux.

Upstream reaches

Fish from its source downstream to the village of Arzenc-de-Randon, here the channel resembles a modest stream flowing over coloured granite aggregate supporting small trout. Try using a sauterelle - grasshopper as hook bait in summer.

Middle reaches

At Arzenc-de-Randon the brook broadens by losing speed in contact with pasture, wetlands and flats. Within 12 km the river is a succession of meanders down to the Pont de Braye. At this point the river is a superb place to dry fly-fish for trout and grayling. Au toc also works well at this location but anglers who prefer spinning should seek out faster water.

Downstream reaches

From the Pont de Braye the gradient increases and the river becomes wilder. The valley becomes narrower entering gorges and the banks are wooded.

The channel that feeds water into the barrage de Naussac situated upstream of Auroux, takes much of the flow which improves downstream of Atger where it is joined by the Grandrieu River. The restricted flow encourages anglers to use dry fly techniques or insectes naturels.

From the start of spring the current is very strong it enables au toc or spinning to achieve results. Two tributaries worth a mention are the Clamouse and Grandrieu Rivers that join the Chapeauroux River respectively at Pont de Braye and downstream of Atger.

Altier River – Mont Lozère

What characterises the river most is its clarity so it is hard to gauge the depth of the pools in the granite rock. A Mediterranean type river its spates are as significant as its dry periods. Trout thrive here.

The Allier, classified as 1st category has its source beneath the summit of Finiels the tallest point in Lozère at 1699 m above sea level situated in the middle of Mont-Lozère, these are granite hills.

Descending from here it follows a narrow valley covered by shale, before flowing 30 km below into the retenue de Bayard-Villefort that supports very large trout some of which head upstream along the Altier River to spawn.

The huge pebbles that make up most of the riverbed offer plenty of cover for trout that average 25-28 cm in length on the downstream reaches along with minnows and large gudgeon.

A significant population of chub originating from the retenue swim upstream for a kilometre along the Altier River: until the impassable dam.

Réserves de Pêche: 400m stretch of the Altier River situated at Altier, fish from 50 m upstream of the passerelle – footbridge downstream to the pont du Château du Champ.

Upstream reaches

Fishing is encouraged from the wetland area near its source around Mont Lozère where the brook takes its time crossing. It then passes along a coniferous forest and after cascades through a tight granite gorge until reaching the village of Cubières. A small torrent, the Altier River supports lots of hard fighting small trout that succumb to au toc, worms and small spinners.

Middle reaches

From Cubières the river gets wider and flows at a steady rate as it enters a valley made from shale whilst still retaining some vigour. The banks are consistently wooded and encourage natural baits or artificial lures, downstream to the hamlet of Rochettes-Basses. Dense vegetation in places and forestation means that casting is restricted and the river at this point is recommended for experienced fly-fishermen.

Downstream reaches

From Rochettes-Basses until the start of the retenue de Villefort the river takes on a Mediterranean character. The occasionally wild rapids in the pothole caverns alternate with tranquil and deep stretches that attract bathers in summer, often to the detriment of fishing. At these busy times anglers are best served by morning and evening sessions.

The deep holes that locals call marmites de sorcières – witches' lairs often contain large trout that have swum upstream from the lake during spring floods.

All fishing techniques work well but remember that the water is very clear except when in flood so use light tackle. Lastly the river is great for dry fly-fishing with a nymph, spotting trout in the water as you walk along the bank.

It's interesting to note that the Altier River at its exit into the retenue de Villefort has no interest to trout anglers due to its slow flow. A little later a small tributary the Palhère River where the current is also limpid houses some beautiful trout. The reservoir has some very large trout that sometimes head up the Altier River to spawn.

Fishing is recommended a little further upstream in the vicinity of Maison Blanche. From Villefort take the D 901. Afer Castanet comes Maison Blanche. Descend along hairpin bends through an orchard. Park up: by the side of the road. By the exit to Cubières the Altier broadens out but narrows again as it enters the gorge. The banks are wooded and fly anglers might like to try further downstream where there is more room to cast. But just upstream before the dam wall there are many anglers using the bait method.

Anglers willing to brave canyon or abseil style fishing should try the tributary Chassezac River situated a little way before the retenue de Pied de Borne in the middle of this area there are impressive gorges. The flow of the Chassezac River is partly controlled upstream by hydroelectric dams. Water regulation also applies to the Borne River the last tributary of the Altier River situated in the south west of the Lozere département.

The Borne River forms the border with the Ardèche départment and when a dam was created upstream a short while ago fishermen stopped visiting. This break has created good fish stocks. The channel runs through gorges that create a good atmosphere.

Granite cliffs at the confluence of the three rivers situate the village called Pied de Borne. The rivers are called the Altier, Borne and Chassezac. Leave the village take a right turn for St Jean D 51 road without crossing the dam. After 1.2 km: on a local road park up by houses and walk down to the river along a path beside a field.

You will arrive at a bridge. From here start fishing upstream where there are several runs. The challenging terrain means that few bother to fish here and because the trout are not used to visitors a stealthy approach brings rewards. After 50 minutes of walking there is a large gorge where the channel is between 4 m and 5 m deep and contains trout up to 35 cm long. 200 m upstream the river splits into smaller channels, the left one is the best. Danile Laurent a local fishing guide recommends light grey sedge fly lures and the wbo to catch some really wild brown trout.

Angling licences: Agence Postale, 48800 Pied de Borne Tel, 0466698015. Restaurant Chez Fernand, 9 place Bosquet, 48800 Villefort Tel, 0466468138. Barrial Louis, articles de pêche, 48800 Villefort Tel, 0466697740.

The Chassezac River is well known for its impressive gorges. Fishing is recommended in the vicinity of Rachas and Prévenchères. Take the D 906 from Villefort to Albespeyres by the viewpoint. Descend to the foot of the dam wall then follow the railway line. After the tunnel join the river downstream through trees that you can use for balance because immediately below there is 400 m of steep slope.

Fishing starts just a bit downstream and ends by the dam. Cliffs tightly box in the canyon and anglers are advised not to fish alone for safety reasons. The riverbed is made up of flagstones, rollers and large boulders that trout find shelter behind. An old bridge spans the river further upstream at the halfway point along this stretch. From here on the river is easier going and the banks have more room to cast. Boats frequent these gorges from June through September. It is then best to fish early morning or later in the day. The best time to fish is from spring until the middle of June.

Angling licences: Café National, Place du Portalet, Villefort 48800 Tel, 0466469726. Bar Restaurant Le Garlaban, Villefort 48800 Tel, 0466468880. Quincaillerie Madame Cauchois, Articles de pêche - Villefort 48800 Tel, 0466697740.

Lac Bayard classified as 1st category and supplies water for Villefort. It is famous for its large fish. And holds the trout record for eastern France. The retenue EDF du lac Bayard is known locally as Lac de Villefort. There is easy access to the shore. Especially: via the bridge by the dam wall. From Villefort take the D 906 through Prévenchères towards Langogne, parking is provided by the turn-off for the lake.

The lake supports brown and rainbow trout, chub and minnows. In 1998 a large head of cristivomer – lake trout were introduced. Trout here attain very good weights easily reaching between 3 kg and 5 kg. The record for this venue stands at 14.3 kg, 1.3 m long and 66 cm in circumference. But local anglers say that even bigger fish avoid capture

Tactics during the day involve using a bombette to catch larger specimens deeper down in combination with a small lure to gain casting distance. At dusk the big fish visit the borders to feed on small fry. The favourite method is the teigne au buldo – bubble float with a moth imitation fly lure. Further along the road are good angling locations including the plans d'eau du Rachas, Roujanel and Béal

Office de Tourisme de Villefort, Rue de l'Eglise,
48800 Villefort Tel, 0466468730 fax: 0466468533
Email: otsi-villefort48@wanadoo.fr www.villefort.free.fr

Jonte River

The gorges of the Jonte River, classified as 1st category are less well known than the Gorges du Tarn where it enters at Rozier after carving through the southwest edges of the Causse Méjean above there glide vultures that were introduced in 2003. They are a sight worth watching.

The Jonte River starts roughly 1.2 km above sea level on the northern slopes of the Massif de l'Aigoual in the very south of the Lozère département. Originating from metamorphic rock it is still a small brook as it flowsby Meyrueis.

The channel widens past Meyrueis accepting water from tributary rivers Brèze and Béthuzon before entering the beautiful gorges mentioned previously that continue for another 22 km until its confluence at Rozier with the Tarn River.

Significant calcium content in the water encourages the growth of aquatic fauna. The trout therefore have a beautiful livery, displaying a striped pattern along its flank similar to those trout found in the larger limestone rivers. The Jonte River contains the highest density of fish per cubic metre of water found in France this also includes minnows and gudgeon.

Upstream reaches

Its source is in vicinity of Gatuzière where initially it's small brook fishing method is au toc, thereafter it evolves into a larger well oxygenated mountain brook with excellent spawning grounds until Meyrueis. And where there are gaps in the wooded banks fly-fishing is worth a go.

Downstream reaches

Fishing is possible in the gorges de la Jonte located from Meyrueis downstream to Rozier. According to local expert fly angler Daniel Laurent the town of Douzes makes a great base for this section of river. Stay at the hotel restaurant that has a trout for its sign. See below for details.

The beautiful river carves into cliff faces along its flanks and gathers in force as it descends between limestone blocks of different sizes eroding volcanic rock in rapid zones and gravel bottoms where it's deeper.

Similar to upstream stretches the multitude of aquatic fauna makes fly-fishing very productive in spring. However dry fly-fishing with a nymph is a bit more complicated because of the fish reflections against the mineral bedrock makes trout harder to spot. Baetis Rodanis – large dark olve dun imitations prove very rewarding early in the season.

Spinning is especially effective for catching larger trout patrolling the faster current found in the gorges. Minnow imitation lures work wonders here. Whatever the angling technique remember that the less noise you make the better your chances of bagging up. Please note that in dry summer months the channel goes underground at Meyrueis reappearing 8 km downstream just upstream of Douzes.

Accommodation and licences: Articles et/ou cartes de pêche: Hôtel restaurant de la Jonte, 48150 Les Douzes Tel, 0565626052.
Agence postale, 48150Le Rozier Tel, 0566626022
Local angling club: Compagnie des guides de pêche Tel, 0466484848

Lot River

An innovation for the 2005 season was the introduction of zones de piedmont where the stocking of robust rainbow trout occurs. These zones include the Tarn River at Quézac à Prades and the Lot River downstream of Chanac, where coarse fish compose 95% of the fish population.. As a whole brown trout occupy 99% of the rivers in Lozère département.

The Lot is the most important river in the département flowing 95 km in Lozère from east to west past Mendea a town recognised as the fishing capital of the region. It links two distinct geographical and geological lowland areas. In the south: the Cévennes and Grandes Causses - Méjean and Sauveterre the stocking of robust rainbow trout. To the north: the Margeride and Aubrac Rivers.

The Lot's source occurs at 1.2 km above sea level on the southern face of the montagne du Goule. Flowing 95 km through Lozère département across three distinct rock patterns. Shale: granite and limestone. In particular amongst volcanic rock between Bagnols-les-Bains and Mende the river encourages a fast growing trout population.

In particular a 30 km stretch that begins to the east upstream at Bagnols-les-Bains downstream to Chanac offers some superb angling sport.

Common grayling were introduced in 2000 around Chanac. They mingle with barbel, chub and dace in good numbers. The Lot River in Lozère département is classified as 1st category. Compared with upland rivers the trout season here lasts longer.

Réserves de Pêche: 650 m stretch of the Lot River stuated at Bagnols les Bains: fish from the confluence with the Riou Frech downstream to the confluence with the ruisseau de la Valettte.

Upstream reaches

A short stretch of 2-3 km with its source in a beech and coniferous forest downstream to the village of Bleymard. It's a modest brook at this point Fishing au toc in small ravines is the way to go here.

Middle reaches

Fish from the village of Bleymard the channel widens after the contribution from the ruisseau de Combe Sourde where the river is confined by a narrow beech lined shale valley. Slippery slate stones form the channel bed.

Between Chadenet and Sainte-Hélène the river flows on granite rock and here the gradient gets considerably steeper. It carves through a deep granite gorge where the current is wild and fast. From Sainte-Hélène until Mende the Lot River plots a calmer course. Rapids alternate with calmer stretches and a deep gorge.

The riverbed is composed of boulders, gravel and granite sand and increasingly limestone. With the exception of upstream areas the Lot River offers the angler a wide range of terrain and different aquatic conditions. All fishing techniques will do well. Even though most of the banks are wooded the wide channels make wading easy.

Downstream reaches

Fish from Mende to the border of the département: downstream from Canourgue exists roughly 50 km of river fishing. The channel becomes wider but retainsa variety of different swims.

Enlarged by the Bramont River, pretty but very calcium rich 7 km downstream from Mende the water at first is clear becoming cloudier and holding more silt.

The second tributary in importance the Colagne River it joins at Ajustons injecting a second breath and an increase in power especially so because of the narrow valley here.

The channel is rich in calcium and nutrients fostering a good trout population the larger specimens are caught using minnow lures. However it possible to bag beautiful trout specimens up to 1 kg using a fly at dusk or try using a spinner in faster well oxygenated current.

The river also lends itself to long range casting with nymphs. Finally for a few kilometres upstream and downstream of Channac there are plenty of common grayling and unlike other French rivers are often caught on a dry fly - the cloudy waters prevents effective nymph fishing by sight.

The Lot is a neasygoing river where trout fishing is most reliable given its consistent nature. Its downstream reaches exist at a lower altitude than is average for the département therefore the effective fishing season begins earlier than other rivers in the region.

Parcours sans tuer – catch and release stretches

Only fly-fishing using barbless hooks is allowed in these areas that are well signposted and controlled by local angling clubs in cooperation with the AAPPMA - national French angling federation.

These areas are free to fish provided that the angler is in pocession of the angling licence required for fishing 1st category waters. The advantage for the environment is that fish are always returned safely therefore natural propagation is encouraged and spawning grounds are protected. The French angling federation sees this is as the future of game fishing in France.

At present less than 1% of the 2,700 km of waterway in Lozère are organised on a catch and release basis. However this proportion will increase and ensure the survival and success of the native brown trout. Areas to fish are as follows.

Alignon River at Pont de Montvert. Fish for three kilometres from: Pont de Vernets downstream to the confluence with the Tarn River. In this river carved into granite rock made up of a succession of calmer basins punctuated by faster water there are four catch and release zones run by the local angling club called AAPPMA de la Haute Vallée du Tarn. For further advice please contact local fishing guide: Pascal Vernier - Tel: 0466458250.

Local angling club Association de Pêche de Langogne has created a catch and release 1.5 km stretch on the Allier River downstream from the pont de Allier RN 88 at Langogne. It contains brown trout and grayling. For more information contact: Antonio Munoz - Morangiès - 48800 Pourcharesses. www.assopeche.com/villefort

Bédaule River: at Fournels. Organised by local angling club Association de Pêche La Gaule Barrabande, fishing from village of Fournels along a 400 m stretch containing lovely brown trout. Fish from the passerrelle du tennis - footbridge: downstream to the pont de la Vachellerie. Contact: Serge Fargier - Tel: 0466316623.

Bès River by the Station Thermale de La Chaldette situated on the Aubrac plateau well known for its cows, cheeses, knives and hard winters. The reserve is set up in cooperation with local angling club Fédération de Pêche Cantalienne fish along an 800 m stretch situated from upstream of the pont de la Chalderette to the right of the Station Thermale. Contact: Serge Fargier – Tel, 0466316623.

Colagne River: at Marvejols - Chirac. A catch and release fishing reserve was established here in 1991. It's not just the oldest but also the longest at 2.5 km. Located immediately downstream of Marvejols, fish from the digue des Tanneries downstream to the Passerelle du Besset - footbridge situated in Chirac. Fishing is good at dusk. Contact: Christian Oddoux - Tel: 0466320562.

Gourdouze River at Vialas. Maintained by local angling club AAPPMA des Hautes Vallées du Tarn and Luech the fishing reserve is situated in the middle of the Parc National des Cévennes. A 600 m stretch situated upstream of the hamlet called Gourdouze. Contact: Pascal Vernier - Tel. 0466458250. Denis Mazoyer - Tel. : 0466410115.

Jonte and Béthuzon River at Meyrueis. Situated at the confluence of the two rivers in the middle of the pretty village of Meyruies along a 900 m stretch. Please note that the brown trout spawn late here so please avod wading into spawning grounds. Contact: Yannick Arnal - Tel: 0466456211.

Langouyrou River: at Langogne. There is a large population of brown trout here. In spite of the short length of the resrve at 250 m you will have fun. Fish from the pont Nuef: downstream to the pont du parking. Contact: Eric Moulin – Tel: 0466690267. And on the Allier River for a 1.5 km stretch situated at Langogne from downstream of the Pont de Allier (RN 88).

Lot River at Bagnols-les-Bains. There are two catch and release fishing reserves located here. The first stretch is 350 m long crossing the village of Bagnols Les Bains-Chadenet situated 100 m upstream of the Pont du Casino and anglers are asked to respect spawning areas located here. The second reserve was established in 1996 and is situated from upstream of the confluence with the ruisseau de Valette by the east end of the public campsite. To downstream of the Pont de Crouzet along a 1 km stretch. Contact: Marius Tournaire – Tel: 0466651525.

Lot River at Mende. A 1.4 km stretch situated in the middle of town between the Pont de Paulin Daudé and the Pont Notre-Dame. There are lots of very big brown trout present here. It's especially good at dusk. Contact: Marius Tournaire - Tel: 0466651525.

Lot and Bramont Rivers at Balsièges. The reserve is maintained by local angling club Association Agréée de Pêche de Balsièges-Valdonnez. Brown trout are present in one of the most beautiful resreves in the Lozère they are are in excellent condition at the confluence of the two rivers. The stretch is 1.3 km long and runs along RN 88 and RN 106 roads, there is good access to the channels along the whole of the bank. Contact : Stéphane Cournac - Tel: 0685745776. Pierre Vlahovitch - Tel: 0466470260.

Lot River at Chanac – Chateau de ressouches. Easy access: with an impressive backdrop. 850 m stretch. Fish from the digue de Moulin Grand: downstream to the pont Vieux – old bridge. Local angling club La Loutre Chanacoise maintains a 1 km reserve. Contact: Claude Bergman - Tel: 0615145207.

Ruisseau de Rieutord at Vialas. 1.2 km stretch maintained by local angling club AAPPMA des Hautes Vallées du Tarn and Luech on a tributary of the Luech River. Situated upstream from Vialas on the RN 998 road where a road bridge forms the upstream border of the fishing reserve. The downstream border is by the confluence with the Luech River. Brown trout are caught to good sizes. Contact : Pascal Vernier - Tel: 0466458250. Denis Mazoyer - Tel: 0466410115.

Remeize River at Lile des Bessons. A tributary of the Aubrac River: that meanders gently along evoking pleasant memories and future hopes for all anglers in the Lozère. Sometimes placid but often fast running. A 1.5

km stretch, the fishing reserve was established in 2001. It is situated between the villages of Lile and Bessons, roughly 3 km from Saint Chély, Aumont Aubrac and Fau de Peyre. Contact: Serge Fargier - Tel: 0466316623.

Tarn River at Pont de Montvert. The fishing reserve was established in 2002 by local angling club AAPPMA de la Haute Vallée du Tarn. This is a 1 km stretch situated from upstream of Pont Romain until the confluence with the ruisseau de la Mérede l'Aygue this forms the upstream boundary. Contact: Pascal Vernier - Tel. 0466458250.

Tarn River at Pont de Montvert. The fishing reserve is situated across the village of Pont de Montvert along a 250 m stretch upstream of the confluence with the Rieumalet River. Anglers here will fall under the eye of inquisitive tourists. Contact: Pascal Vernier - Tel: 0466458250.

Tarn River on 1 km stretch in vicinity of Pont de Montvert from the confluence with the Ru de la Mère de l'Aygue.

Tarn River: at Bédouès. The fishing reserve is situated between the Pont de la Vernède and the confluence with the ravin de la Combe along a 2.2 km stretch. This is one of the most attractive locations to fish in Lozère. It is the second fishing reserve established by local angling club AAPPMA de la Haute Vallée du Tarn with help from the Bédouès-Cocurès branch of the angling club. The reserve runs by the Château de Miral and no angler leaves disappointed. Contact: Pascal Vernier - Tel: 0466458250. Maurice Ramade - Tel.: 0466452133.

Tarn River: at Saint-Julien-du-Gourg and Florac. 1.2 km stretch maintained by local angling club APPMA 'La Floracoise. The fishing reserve is situated: by the village of Saint-Germain-du-Gourg the downstream border is by the Pont-de-Fayet. This stretch of the Tarn River is quite shallow with wide channels it waschosen with fly-fishermen in mind. Contact: Daniel Brunel – Tel: 0466451549.

Tarn River at Laval-du-Tarn and Sainte-Énimie situated within the estates of the Château de la Caze. The fishing reserve is situated in the majestic Gorges du Tarn: by the imposing backdrop formed by the Château de la Caze. A 1.5 km stretch populated by wild brown trout that attain a good size. The location offers a series of superb swims. Magic. Contact: René Couderc - Tel: 0466485007.

Tarn-Jonte fishing reserve, Alignon River, on 2 km stretch: in the vicinity of Pont de Montvert-St Maurice Ventalon. Fish from: the pont de Vernets. Bethuzon River on 400 m stretch in vicinity of Meyrueis from the pont de Mars. Jonte River on 500 m stretch in vicinity of Meyruies from the confluence with the Brèze River. Tarn River on 1 km stretch in vicinity of Pont de Montvert from the confluence with the Ru de la Mère de l'Aygue. Tarn River on 250 m stretch in vicinity of Pont de Montvert upstream of the confluence. Tarn River on 2.2 km stretch in vicinity of Bedous from the pont de Vernède. Tarn River on 1.2 km stretch in vicinity of Florac from upstream of the pont de Fayet. Tarn River on a 1.5 km stretch in vicinity of Laval du Tarn-Ste Enimie in the grounds of the Chateau de la Caze.

Truyère River: at Saint-Léger-du-Malzieu. This is a river with a European wide reputation. She symbolises the Margeride. Situated 3 km downstream from Malzieu: known locally as the Perle de la Vallée. A 300 m stretch: by the village of Saint-Léger-du-Malzieu. Fish from the pont de la D 75: downstream to the confluence with the Chambaron. At this location the channel runs amongst large boulders surrounded by hills covered in pine forest. Contact: Serge Fargier - Tel: 0466316623.

Altier-Chassezac fishing reserve on Altier River. 1.1 km stretch in vicinity of Altier-Pourcharesses: fish downstream from the digue de Combret.

Bethuzon River on 400m stretch in vicinity of Meyrueis from the pont de Mars.

AAPPMA Canton de Villfort (48)
Mr Antonio Munoz: Président
48800
Pourcharesses
Tel: 0466461963
villefort@assopeche.com

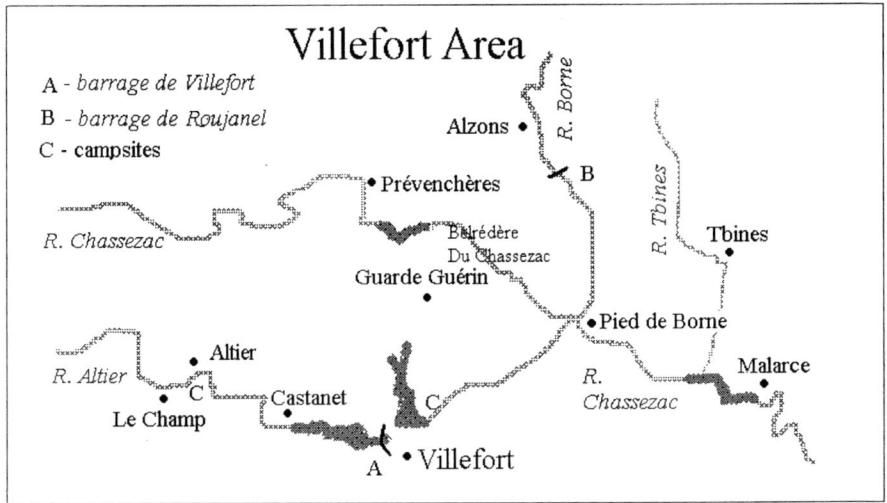

The lakes

The lakes in the Aubrac have dark coloured water that contrasts with the deep and wild fishing reserves found in the reservoirs to the east of the département. Anglers can catch, trout, pike, perch, chub and various coarse fish.

Natural lakes found in the Aubrac

Lac des Salhiens: (6 ha), Lac Saint-Andéol (11 ha), Lac de Born (5 ha), Lac de Souverols (1,6 ha). These four lakes are situated on the plateau de l'Aubrac at an average altitude of 1250 m above sea level. They are equidistant from each other and of a similar nature and all are found in the Bès River basin. These are: strongly tinted waters, the banks are regularly cut back but they tend to be hard to walk along due to the spongy and moving nature of the ground. The lakes are classified as 1st category; the best angling techniques include spinning with a spoon, rapala or minnow imitation. Or fly-fishing: using streamers imitation flylures. Fishing on Lac de Salhiens and Saint Andéol is private. Contact the département angling federation for advice.

Reservoirs

Plan d'eau de Booz (9 ha) situated in the Lot River valley between Canourgue and Chirac. A lovely place to visit: and fish.

Lac du Ganivet (12 ha) situated in the Aubrac-Margeride on the upper reaches of the Colagne River 1444 m above sea level, this small shallow lake supports some pretty trout from the river and some gudgeon and minnows. Classified as 1st category it's best-fished using worm, artificial lures and fly.

There is no fishing permitted at **Lac de Charpal** (190 ha).

Lac du Moulinet (13 ha). Situated near the A75 road 1075 m above sea level it collects water from the Crueize River before the river enters the vallée de l'enfer - valley of hell. Shallow and classified as 1st category it supports rainbow and brown trout, pike, perch, tench, chub and small coarse fish found in running water. Spinning: or worming works well here.

Lac de Naussac (1050 ha) situated in the Allier valley. It is the biggest water in the dèpartement and is water control for the Allier River. It offers loads of places to fish that are immediately accessible exiting from the RD 26 road that borders one side of the reservoir. The wilder opposite bank has several cuts where feeder streams enter. There are rainbow trout and some nice brown trout specimens along with dace, perch and unfortunately increasingly invasive chub and roach. Many anglers fish at depth with worms to catch perch. Fly-fishing gets results for large chub and rainbow trout from the cleared shoreline.

In the Cévenoles valleys are found four lakes.

Lac de Bayard-Villefort (136 ha) Altier River
Lac du Rachas (53 ha) Chassezac River
Lac de Roujanel (41 ha) Borne River
Lac de Pied de Borne (60 ha)

These lakes are a series of reservoirs designed for hydroelectric power generated by the dam on the Pied de Borne reservoir. All the lakes are classified in 1st category and are stocked with brown and rainbow trout, dace and chub. Lac de Villefort has been stocked with cristivomer after it was drained in 1988. Here the trout grow big, many are caught over 5 kg and it holds the French record for a rainbow trout at 14.3 kg.

Lac de Puylaurent

All of these lakes produce hydroelectric power for the EDF plant at Pied-de-Borne. Situated respectively on the Altier, Chassezac and Borne Rivers and they all present with the exception of upstream floods a gentle character that reflects the shale colour of these valleys.

Steepinclines often make access to the banks difficult, which in turn are sometimes unstable and access roads are sometimes a distance from the rivers including the Roujanel.

All are classified as 1st category. And all support rainbow and brown trout, dace and chub. Lac de Bayard-Villefort also supports a population of cristivomers – lake trout introduced after the water was drained in 1988. It's worth noting that the brown trout can reach extraordinary weights and sizes. Exceptional: even for these lakes. Especially in Bayard-Villefort where the middle reaches is the best place to fish exceeding 5 kg and even above 14.3 kg a French national record.

Fishing with imitation minnow lures works wonders otherwise use large spoon lures. The barrages de Puylaurent and Roujanel have limited fishing due to significant changes in the water level due to HEP activity that makes any sort of fish management ill advised.

Parcours de Pêche Touristiques – tourist fishing stretches

There are three places to fish that have especially been created as safe and family friendly lakes with good access and green banks. Free angling tuition is provided for beginners and kiddies.

- Étang de la Bastide, situated in the east of the département Tel, 0466460140 / 0466653611
- Étang de Saint Léger du Malzieu situated to the north Tel, 0466317579 / 0466653611
- Étang de Barrandon situated in the centre on Mont Lozère Tel, 0466653611

The first two lakes are open from the 30th April at weekends and public holidays until the 30th June from 9 a.m. till noon then from 2 p.m. till 7 p.m. From the 1st July through the 3rd Sunday in September they are open every day same hours.

The étang de Barrandon is open from the 14th May to the third Sunday in September every day same hours as the other two lakes. Fly-fishing instruction takes place here. There is also a fishermen's hut for walkers where you will need to bring your own firewood to manage the stove. Half-day tickets are available on site, €10.5 for 5 trout, €19 for ten trout, €2 for every extra trout.

Etang de Bonnecombe: this lake is run along similar lines to the last three but is managed by the Syndicat Intercommunal de l'Aubrac-Cologne. Situated on the Col de Bonnecombe along the road from St Germain du Teil to Nasbinals. For opening times and regulations contact the Mairie de St Germain du Teil – town hall Tel, 0466326016.

Plan d'eau de Truyere: opened for the first time in spring 2000 it covers 10 hectares and is situated directly upstream of the village of Malzieu-Vile near to tourist accommodation. The lake is stocked with good quality rainbow and brown trout specimens reaching 1-½ kilos. For details contact: Fédération de Pêche a Mende tel, 0466653611 or contact the Mairie du Malzieu-Ville Tel, 0466317025.

Ecoles de Pêche de Lozère – fishing schools are not just for kiddies

At Florac, Mr Brunel, Tel, 046645154939, Av Jean Monestier 48400 Florac, open February to June, on Saturdays from 9a.m. till noon, fly-fishing taught to beginners, age range taught from 8-16 years and adults.

At Langogne, Mr Bonhomme Tel, 046660613, Avenue de la Tour 48300 Naussac and Mr Bouvier, Tel, 0466460303, 48250 Rogleton, open February through June on Fridays from 5.30p.m. till 7p.m. fly-fishing taught for age groups from 8-16 years and adults. Beginners and intermediate.

At Villefort, Mr Munoz, Tel, 0466461963, Morangiès 48800 Pourcharesses, open from Marc hthrough June, on Saturdays, from 2p.m. till 5p.m. fly-fishing taught for age group 8-16 years old.

At Pont de Montvert, Mr Vernier, Tel, 0466458250, Le Mazel 48220 Le Pont de Montvert, open from March though June on Saturdays from 2p.m. till 5p.m. techniques taught include fly-fishing, bait fishing, spinning, carp fishing and float. For ages: 8-16. Beginners and intermediate.

At Mende, Mr Tournaire, Tel, 0466651525, 34 lot églantiers 48000 Mende, open from March through June on Wednesday from 2p.m. till 4p.m. float and bait fishing taught to beginners and fly –fishing taught to intermediate, 8-16 year olds.

At Balsièges, Mr Cournac, Tel, 0466323161, Charamaude 48100 Palhers, open from March though June on Fiday from 5p.m. till 7p.m. bait fishing taught to beginners and Saturday from 9a.m. till noon. Fly-fishing taught to intermediates. 8-16 years of age and adults.

Where to obtain day tickets and angling licences?

❖ 5 Rue de la Libertè, 48000 Mende Tel, 0466651492
❖ 54 Av. Jean Monestier, 48400 Florac Tel, 0466450317
❖ Restaurant 9 place Bosquet, 48800 Villfort Tel, 0466468138
❖ Buffet de la Gare, Place de la Gare, 48300 Langogne Tel, 0466690114
❖ Tabac Loto, 38 Rue Théophile Roussel, 48200 St Chély d'Apcher Tel, 0466310306
❖ Bar Tabac La Barrière, Av. Théo Roussel, 48100 Marvejols Tel, 0466321139
❖ Le Moulin d'Olt Montjézieu, 48500 LA Canourge Tel, 0466326144
❖ Café du Progrès, 48260 Nasbinals Tel, 0466325140
❖ Café du Commerce, 48220 Le pont de Montvert Tel, 0466458019
❖ Hotel Restaurant Bargeton, 48190 Cubières Tel, 0466486254

ARIÈGE 09

Ariège is situated on the border with Spain at the foot of the Pyrenees. It is landlocked with the Pyrénnées Orientales to the east, the Aude and Haute Garonne to the north and the Hautes-Pyrénées to the west.

The Fédération de l'Ariège was founded in 1922 it represents 45 local angling clubs and 10,000 licensed anglers. It controls 3,200 km of rivers including 2,700 km in 1st category and 1,700 hectares of lakes, 900 hectares in 1st category. There are over 200 mountain lakes to fish.

TheUpper Ariège in particular in particular is a paradise for trout and wildlife. This mountain region is beautiful and wild. Streams and lakes are found everywhere. The water is so clear that trout can be spotted dancing in the stream. Fishing conditions and angling methods do change daily and anglers will never grow bored.

For more information contact:

Fédération de Pêche de l'Ariège
13 Place du 59 ^{ème} R.I.
B.P. 18 09001 Foix - cedex-France
Tel, +33 (0) 5.34.09.31.09. Fax, +33 (0) 5.61.65.12.40. Email: federation@peche-ariege.com

The angling federation clubhouse at the above address is open to everyone weekdays from 8a.m. to noon then again from 1.30p.m. - 6p.m.

Each season the local angling federation uses a helicopter to restock its mountain lakes. This is the most efficient way of reaching the highest mountain tarns. In July 2005 a successful 6 hour round trip introduced 72,000 brown trout fry, 8000 saumon de fontaine, 2000 omble chevalier and 1280 cristivomer fry into half the lakes. The following summer the remainder of the lakes were stocked.

There is a relatively short fishing season on the high altitude lakes. But the choice is there for anglers to fish other lakes and rivers at lower altitude where the season lasts longer. And you don't have to walk as far.

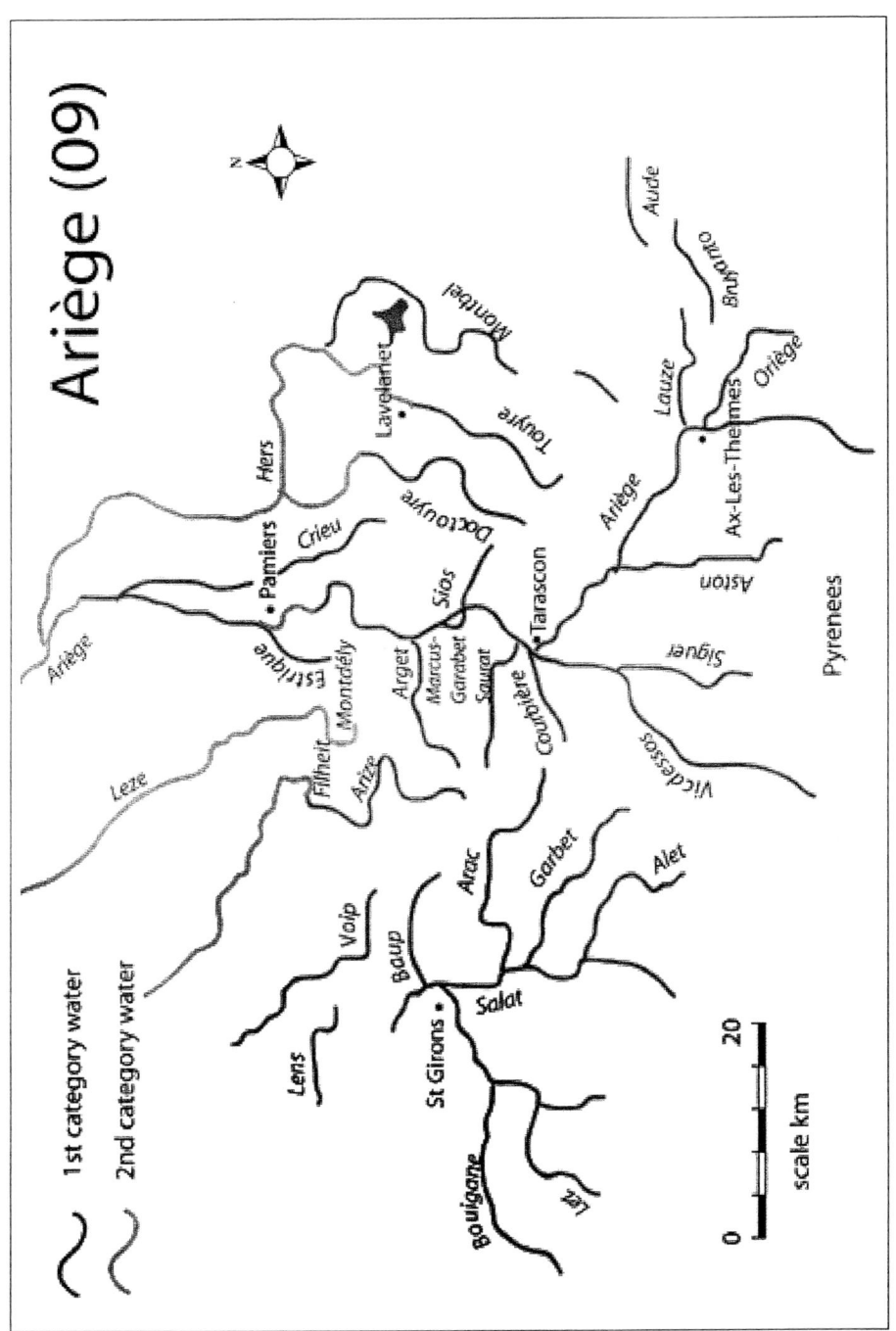

Essentially the Ariège département can be divided into 7 river basins. These are the Couserans, Oust, Vicdessos, Ax-Les Thermes, Orlu, Olmes and Donezan Rivers.

In particular there are 7 baliffs' offices representing the Siege de la Brigade – forming part of the Ministère de l'Ecologie et du Développement essentially they act as bailiffs patrolling the département divided up into these 7 areas.

For more information contact: Siège de la brigade: 13, place du 59ème RI - B.P. 18 - 09001 Foix Cedex – Tel, 0534093824. Email: bd09@csp.ecologie.gouv.fr

Travelling times are given for the mountain lakes mentioned below: These times can seem long, but there is little driving and a lot of walking. So bring your hiking boots and get some fitness training before you arrive, you will need it.

Rules and regulations

Trout fishing season runs from 11th March through 17th September, but you can fish for rainbow trout on 2nd category water all year.

Water over 1000 m above sea level is fishable from 25th May through 17th September but please check the weather before you set out. It may seem very sunny when you set out but things may change rapidly for the worse when you reach the uplands. Be prepared, take some extra clothing and let someone know your expected time of return.

Brown trout and brook trout minimum size is 20cm.
Omble chevalier – 23cm
Cristivomer – 35cm
Rainbow trout – 20cm

There is a 10-bag limit for all trout caught. One rod is permitted on 1st category water two hooks and three flies at most. Fishing is banned for salmon, grayling and sea trout.

Angling licences

Carte complète, annual licence covers all types of water – €62.5
Carte vacances, holiday licence, cover all types of water, valid for any two week period from June to September – €30
Carte jeune, under 16's – €24
Carte jeune, under 12's – €42

Rivers classified as 1st category water - where anglers may catch trout

Ariège River fishing along its whole course in the département with the exception of lac de Labarre and the river stretch surrounding the canal de l'usine hydroélectrique de Pébernat, near Pamiers
Lens River fish from its source until the end of the département
Salat River fish upstream of the pont de Lacave
Hers River fish upstream of its confluence with the river Touyre
Touyre River fish upstream of the outflow pipe of the station d'épuration industrielle du Moulin d'En Four – purifier plant.
Douctouyre River fish upstream of its confluence with the ruisseau de Limbrassac

Arize River fish upstream of its confluence with the ruisseau de Gabre
Aude River fish along its entire course in the département
Volp River fish upstream of its confluence with the ruisseau de Vieille
The ruisseau de Montfa
Tributaries and affluents of all the stretches mentioned above, with the exception of the ruisseaux de Gabre and Limbrassac.

All waters in Ariège are classified as 1st category unless stated otherwise

The French terms étang and lac are interchangeable, both mean lake

A. Oust is a peaceful small village situated in the Pyrenees Ariégeoises, located at the confluence of the Garbet and Salat Rivers in the Haut Couserans between the towns of Couserans and Vicdessos, where one enters by the narrow Kercabanac pass. The sector is next to the Spanish border. From Mount Valier, 2838 m above sea level to the Pic Rouge de Bassiès, 2676m above sea level Three main valleys exist here: the vallée du Salat, vallée de l'Alet - Ustou and the vallée du Garbet. Office du Tourisme Tel, 933) (0) 5 61960001.

Oust-Alet

Étang d'Alet: 1904 m above sea level 17 ha in area 60 m in depth it is one of the deepest lakes in the Pyrenees. It is found at the east end of the pic de la Fourne – 2550 m above sea level. An enormous granite rock face encloses its northern bank and its outfall is negligible.

Étang de la Hilette: 1824 m above sea level, 4 ha, the lake is precariously cut out by a glacier, its name comes from an island or more specifically from a peninsula that divides the lake in two.

Massat

Etang de Lers: 1264 m above sea level 7 ha. Stocked with trout, carte journalière – day ticket costs 10 euros it's sold on site but ad 3 euros if you are not holding a angling licence from this département. Other fish species caught include rainbow trout, roach, dace and perch. The lake is open from 3rd June through 17th September.

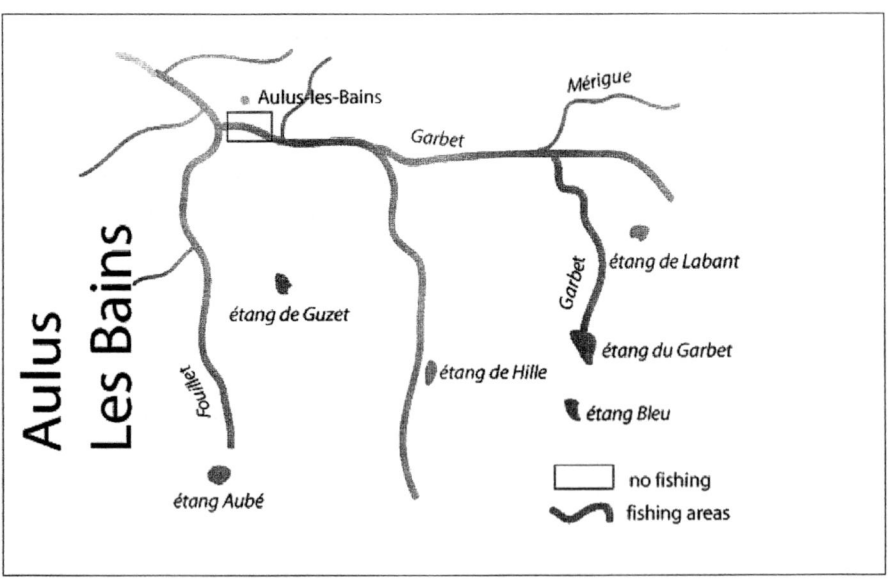

Area controlled by local angling club called La Truite Aulusienne based in Aulus Les Bains.
Contact Jean-Pierre Galin +33 (0) 561960150

Places to fish: ruisseau de Garbet and it tributaries and the lacs du Garbet and Guzet.

Réserves de Pêche – fishing reserves

Ruisseau Garbet around Aulus-les-Bains crossing through the village along a 400 m stretch. From the pont de la route de Lattrape downstream to the first house situated 150 m under the pont des Bains on the right bank.

Purchase your licence at: Tabac Amiel, Aulus les Bains
Tel, +33 (0) 561960436

Local lakes that you can fish, all waters contains trout

Étang de Guzet: 1459 m above sea level. 1.4 ha. The lake is set in a lovely location surrounded by trees just above Aulus les Bains and near the station de ski de Guzet-Neige. Situated at the bottom of a shale depression. It's not that high up.

Etang du Garbet: 15.5 ha 1683 m above sea level. According to the Abbé Gaurier newspaper on July 5, 1921 the neighbouring étang Bleu that is situated higher up was completely frozen. This fact means that the large lac du Garbet, is well fed and its water level can easily be raised, because the lake is retained by a impermeable granite block that is eroded only at the place where the outfall exits. A dam has already been suggested.

The Etang Bleu located above the Etang du Garbet, 1989 m above sea level 1.6 ha and in spite of its altitude is often still frozen rather late in the season. Both waters are situated high up in the mountains.

Lac de Labant covers 0.45 ha

There is a stretch of water reserved for anglers under 16 years of age on the ruisseau Garbet in Aulaus les Bains situated between the pont de Canalus, to downstream along the route de Guzet.

B. The Vallée de Vicdessos located in Ariège, 30 km long, it contains more than sixty lakes. It has survived its isolated location, because of intense industrial activity; iron ore was mined from the middle Ages. Located above Sem, the mine of Rancié was considered in the 18th century century "the largest treasure of the Pyrenees". This mine fed all the forging mills of Ariège until 1931. Hill farming and intensive pastoralism complemented the original activity. Office du Tourisme: Vicdessos Tel, 0561648259. Auzat Tel, 0561648753.

Courbière

The étang d'Artats, or Artax: 1695 m above sea level. 7,5ha is situatedwithin 5 km of the village of Gourbit by the ruisseau d'Artats. Located in the massif des Trois Seigneurs, its location at relatively low altitude makes the lake easily accessible at the beginning of spring and late autumn.

Bassiès

Etang d'Escalès: 1594 m above sea level both waters are situated high up in the mountains. 3.6 ha, lower in altitude than the Etangs de Bassiès. This is a pretty lake but it does not seem to have many fish. Its pleasant banks and acceptable depth somehow make it more hospitable. There are minnows. Little surface activity but there are fishermen.

Etang long: 1624 m above sea level 2.8 ha. Not very deep: and one of the least fished lakes in the Bassiès area. But some nice fish have been spotted at dusk. Moreover, an important waterfall coming from the étang majeur guarantees a stable water temperature and consistent oxygen. level. There are lots of minnows.

The étang majeur: 1639 m above sea level 21 ha is the largest of the étangs de Bassiès, it is very deep and dark but its surface and the direct arrival of water from the cirque which is located above certainly makes this the best lake for fishing. In any case it is the lake that gives the best results with beautiful catches. Many minnows when water temperature is raised.

Etang du Pla de la Fon: 1645 m above sea level 2.9 ha. the lake receives water from the brook that descends from the cirque. It is very flat with a big maraicageuse area that ascends to the angler's refuge hut where small streams have divided from the main channel. Some nice catches occur here but there are some smaller trout are present that have come from the stream.

The étang Mort: 1963 m above sea level 0.9 ha bears its name well because there is no surface activity except for many minnows. The lake is in the course of filling with aquatic vegetation that perhaps hide some brown trout.

The étang de Légunabens: 1655 m above sea level 1 ha. Few anglers visit this lake, it does have a marked out path but few people know that it is there, it best seen in evening when its greenery and its setting give off an incredibly peaceful vibe.
Soulcem

Etangs de Canalbonne sup (Riufret)

Two anonymous lakes situated at 2812 m above sea level 0,3 ha: and 2610m above sea level 0,5 ha situated between the pic de Canalbonne and the pic d'Estats. The third lake situated at 2812 m above sea level has no angling interest its claim to fame is to be the highest lake in the Pyrenees.

The barrage de Soulcem 1570 m above sea level 87 ha was built between 1980 and 1983 by Electricité de France (EDF) the height of dam wall is 78m its length is 275 m and width is 15.m at the top width at the base is 50 m - volume of the dam is 1.642.000 m3 – volume of the retenue is 29.30 hm3. Visitors can park just above Soulcem. In 2003 the reservoir was drained for its 10-year inspection. Electric fishing was carried outto save the fish it saved 500 trout.

The barrage de Soulcem is located at 1570 m above sea level 87 ha at the bottom of the vallée du Vicdessos. Electricité de France (EDF) constructed it between 1980 and 1983. It submerged a vast plateau previously dedicated to farming. Its creation strongly upset the activity of the valley by causing the abandonment of cow breeding. In a geographical sense, the old ways were abandoned with the profit of a road accessible in the car under good conditions up to the Plateau de la Creu. At times, a barrier in point of reception at the end of the lake, makes it possible to limit access to shepherds because the road is deteriorated beyond this point. This makes it possible to give access to many summer and winter excursions for anglers.

The étang de la Soucarrane 2291 m above sea level and 4.3 ha with the foot of the peak of the Red 2902 m above sea level, the port of Roumazet 2571 m above sea level, the port of Bouet and the peak of Médecourbe 2913 m above sea level. Orris are present throughout the Soulcem valley.

The étang d'Izourt is 1647 m above sea level 32.5 ha is accessible via the vallée de l'Arties. This was the site of a catastrophe during the snow-covered spring of 1939 when 28 workmen were killed.

The étang Blaou 2335 m above sea level 16.5 ha is formed in the shape of half-circle, it is bordered in the south-east by cliffs of the peaks of the pics de Bagnets et de Thoumasset at 2,741 m above sea level.

Area controlled by local angling club called La Truite du Montcalm based at Auzat

Contact them at: Maison de Pêche, Anciennes Écoles de Pêche, Rue d'Espagne, 09320, Auzat. Contact Christian Morisse Tel, +33 (0) 561656598.

Places to fish include Vicdessos Riverand its upstream tributaries the Sigeur and Laramade. The ruisseaux de l'Artigue, Artiès, Saleix, Illier, Goulier, Sem and Orus. And the lacs de mointagne -mountain lakes.

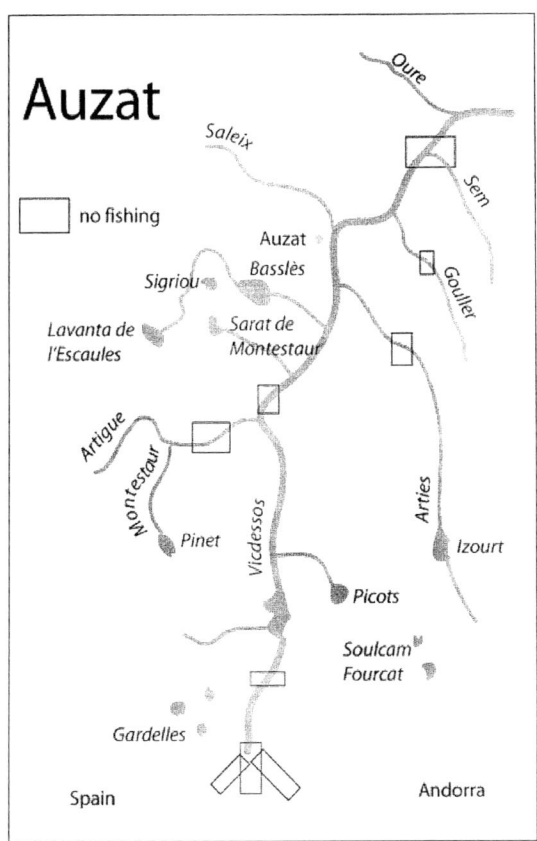

Réserves de Pêche – stocked waters

Vicdessos River fish around Auzat from the pont du centre équestre horse riding centre, downstream to the pont de Capunta.

Ruissea de Monicou near Vicdessos on the plateau de Laminas, fish from 80 m upstream of the pasarelle - footbridge downstream to the head of the waterfalls of Laminas.

Ruisseau de Saleix in vicinity of Auzat, fish from the pont de Barry downstream to the pont du lotissement - housing estate.

Ruisseau du Suc in vicinity of Vicdessos, fish from the micro-central - small power plant downstream to the retenue EDF - lake controlled by EDF watercompany.

Ruisseau de Goulier in vicinity of Goulier, fish from the pont du Moulin - weir/mill pond downstream to the prise d'eau - water intake pipe.

Ruisseau de Sem in vicinity of Sem, fish from the pont del'église - church downstream to the prise de Becquet.

Ruisseau d'Arties in vicinity of Auzat, fish from the passarelle de Balens downstream to the confluence with the Vicdessos River.

Ruisseau du Rat, des Bareytes, du Mounicou and de Médécourbe in vicinity of Auzat on the plateau de la Crouts. Fish from the sources of the tributary streams downstream to the Orri des Estrets.

Etang de Médécourbe; and its feeder streams in vicinity of Auzat.

Purchase your angling licence at: office de tourisme in Auzat Tel, +33 (0) 561648753.

Lakes in the area to fish, most are higher than 2,000 m above sea level.

At Bassiès there are 5 lakes to fish ranging from 0.8 ha to 20.8 ha containing brown trout, rainbow trout and grayling. There is an anglers hut here.

Key: bt – brown trout, cri – cristivomer, gr – grayling, sdf- saumon de fontaine, tac –rainbow trout obl –omble chevalier.

Lac de Caraoussan covers 1.1 ha it contains bt and tac.
Lac de Clots, 0.6ha, bt.
Lac de Crapauds situated towards Mort de Roumazet, 0.4ha,
Lac de Fourcat Grand, 21.7ha, bt and cri.
Lac de Fourcat Petit, 3.85ha, bt, tac
Lac Oussade (Fourcat) 2.9ha.
Lac Gardelle bas (lower), 2.35ha, bt.
Lac Gardelle moyen (middle), 1.5ha, bt, tac
Lac Gardelle haut (upper) 5.8ha, bt and cri
Lac de Goueille, 3.7ha, bt, tac
Lac de Izourt, 31.7ha, bt.
Lac de Lavants des escales, 0.56ha, bt and cri.
Lac de Légunabens 1.05ha, bt.

Lac de Médécourbe, 4.15ha, bt.
Lac de Montestaure, 1.56ha, bt.
Lac de Pestiguer, 1.75ha, bt.
Lac de Picot haute (upper), 1.75ha, bt.
Lac de Picot moyen (middle), 5.75ha, bt.
Lac de Picot bas (lower), 0.3ha, bt.
Lac de Pinet, 0.35ha, bt.
Lac de Rioufret, 2ha, bt.
Lac de Roumazet.
Lac de Sarrat de Montestaure, 0.95ha, bt.
Lac de Sigriou, 1.3ha, bt.
Lac de Soucarrane, 4.4ha, bt.
Lac de Sourd, 1ha, bt.

C. Ax les Thermes is a spa town located in Ariège, built at 720 m above sea level. Ax has 60 natural springs whose temperature varies from 17 to 77 degrees. A public basin in the town centre, allows visitors to take a footbath, this is very soothing after an excursion. Ax les Thermes is also a winter sports resort made up of 3 ski areas: Bonascre, Saquet and Campels these runs are not very wide. They are safe and ideal for families.   Andorra is nearby. On the way is the village of Luzenac, famous for its open talc mines, always in use and close the beautiful Romanesque churches of Axiat and Unac. You can take wonderful day trips and will whitness much wild fauna in the Réserve d'Orlu. Office du Tourisme - vallée d'Ax Tel 0561646060.

Appy

The lac d'Appy 1734 m above sea level 3,8 ha is located in the middle of the massif du St Barthelemi 2348 m above sea level The sun shines all the time on this lake and it thaws out very early in the year. The trout benefit from a longer time to feed up; there are some nice specimens to be caught. In summer it's a popular destination for anglers as are all the lakes with less than a two-hour walk. It is regarded over fished and the trout are considered a bit canny. Some gudgeon are present.

Lause

Barrage de Goulours sur la Lause built in1946. The lake shore is surrounded by trees, and it's not that high up.

Ax Les Thermes

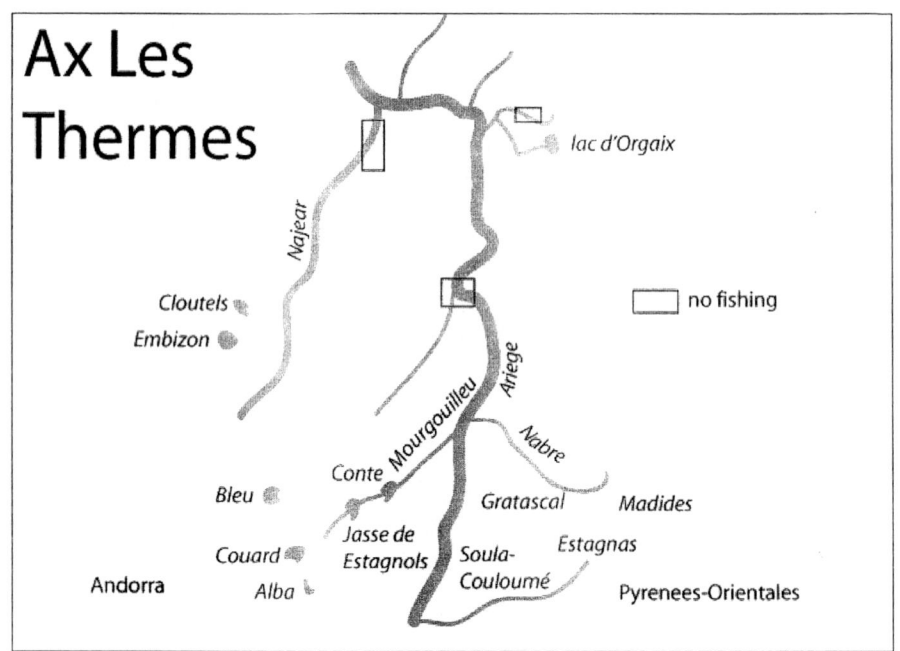

Waters to fish in area controlled by local angling club called la Fario de la Haute Ariège based in Ax les Thermes.

Contact: Jean Louis Fugairon Tel, +33 (0) 561642713.

Places to fish

Ariège River: fish from Bésines to Savignac les Ormeaux. Lauze River: fish along a 2 km stretch situated upstream of Ax-les-Thermes. Oriège River: fish from lac d'Orgeix towards Campauleil until the confluence with the Ariège River.

Résérves de Pêche

Ariège River: in vicinity of Ax-les-Thermes and Merens les Vals for a 600m stretch from the pont Lafford downstream to the Téléphérique - cableway.

Ruisseau de Najear in the vicinity of Savignac les Ormeaux, fish from the cascade de la Failbade - waterfull downstream to the confluence with the river Ariège.

Lauze River in vicinity of Ax-les-Thermes, fish from the pont Noir downstream to the pont de Couzillou.

Purchase your angling licence at Ax Sports in Ax-les-Thermes Tel, +33 (0) 561642177.

Lakes to fish in the area:

Deux lacs d'Albe: l'Albe bas 2295 m above sea level 0.95 ha: and Alba haut 2355 m above sea level 6.75 ha. There are two access routes: one is at the beginning of Mérens-les-Vals via the vallée du Mourguillou, the other from Hospitalet via la vallée de Baldarquès.

Lac de Auriol, 1.2 ha, bt and gr.

The lac des Bésines 1980 m above sea level 6.8 ha is situated at the foot of the pic Pedrous 2842 m above sea level and the pic Auriol 2695 m above sea level. It contains brown trout and has an anglers' hostel.

Barrage de Baldarques 2000 m above sea level 1.4 ha situated above the étang de Pédourres.

Lac de Bleu, 3ha, bt and gr.
Lac de Conte, 3.45ha, bt.
Lac de Cloutels, 1ha, bt.
Lac de Couard, 9.1ha, gr.
Lac de Coume d'Agnel (ru) 0.3ha, bt.
Lac de oume d'Or (font Glacial), 0.5ha, bt.
Lac de Embizop, 4.2ha, bt.
Lac de Estagnas, 0.3ha, bt and tac.

Font Glaciale, 2407 m above sea level 0,25 ha, small lake, lost at the top of Coume d'Or its water flows into the vallée des Bésines, situated opposite the new anglers' refuge, it ends in a pretty waterfall. The lake was stocked 2 years ago.

Lac deGratcasal (3 étangs), 0.3ha, bt and tac.
Lac de Jasse de Estagnols, 0.2ha, bt.
Lac de Jasse de la Parade, 1ha, tac.
Lac de Jasse Pujol, 0.3ha, bt.

Lac de Madides (4 étangs), 2ha, bt and tac.
Lac de Moulsut haut, 0.8ha, bt and tac
Lac de Moulsut bas, 0.3ha, bt and tac.
Lac de Présasse, 0.3ha, bt.
Lac de Soula Couluomé, 1.8ha, bt, gr and tac.

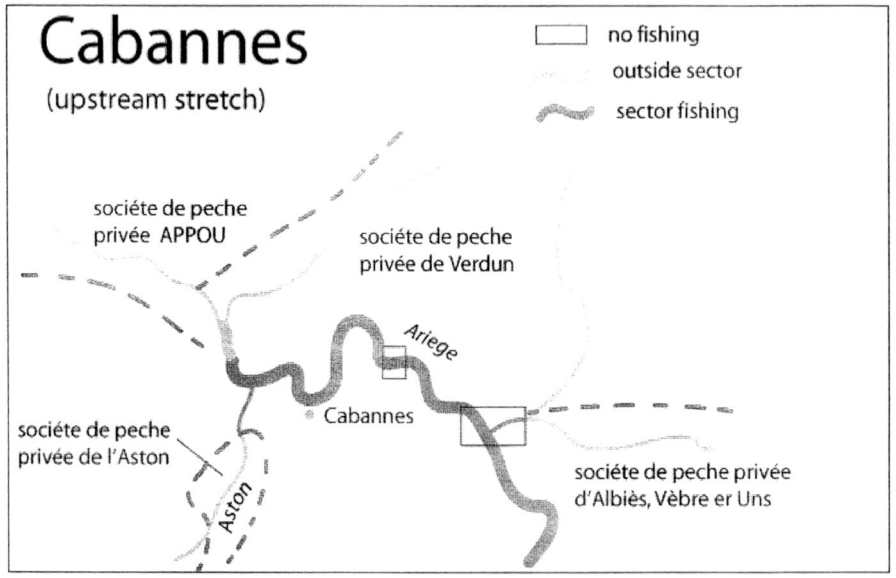

Area controlled by local angling club called La Truite Cabannaise based at Les Cabannes.

Contact: André Del Rio, Tel, +33 (0) 561649897

Areas to fish include river Ariège at Alous until the centrale d'Albiès - power station. Aston River situated at the confluence with the Ariège River fish until the pont de Château-Verdun and upstream of Laparan.

The Ariège River fish in vicinity of Les Cabannes, fish from the digue de la micro-centrale de Foussat - dyke at the mini-power station downstream to the RN20 road bridge.

Canal de la micro-centrale du Foussat, fish from the vannes du canal - lock gate downstream to the confluence with the river Ariège.

Canal de la micro-centrale de Pont Verdun, fish from the vanes du canal - lock gates downstream to the usine - factory.

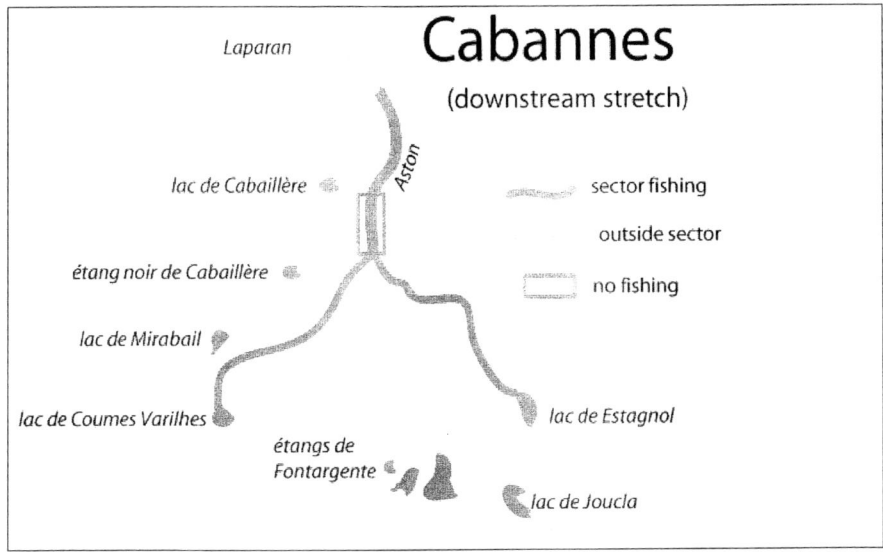

Aston River in vicinity of Aston, fish from the confluence with the Coume de Varilhes River downstream to the déversoir - spillway of the étang de la Caballière.

Purchase your angling licence at: office de tourisme des Cabannes Tel, +33 (0) 561649898. And tabac presse called Marfain in Cabannes Tel, +33 (0) 561649898.

Lakes worth fishing

Lac de Caballière, 2.5ha, bt, tac, sdf, cris
Lac de Coumes Varilhes, 0.8ha, bt, tac, sdf, cris
Lac de Estagnoles des Jonces, 0.4ha, bt, tac, sdf, cris
Lac de Fontargente Grand, 16.9ha, bt, tac, sdf, cris
Lac de Fontargente Moyen (middle lake), 5.6ha, bt, tac, sdf, cris
Lac de Joucla (3 étangs), 5.7ha, bt, tac, sdf, cris
Lac de Larnoum, 2.1ha, bt, tac, sdf, cris Anglers' refuge on site.
Lac de Mirabail, 2.6ha, bt, tac sdf, cris

D. Located in Ariège, Couserans is a country of mountains, hills, meadows, lakes, waterfalls and forests. Among its 18 valleys located at the foot of majestic Mont Valier found 2838 m above sea level some locations remained isolated until quite recently this enabled them to preserve a unique character for instance the Vallée de Bethmale. St Lizier is worth a visit on your day off. Office de Tourisme du Couserans Tel, 0561962660.

Etang d'Araing: 1965 m above sea level 33 ha, depth is 25 m, 1 km long, the EDF replaced an old dam here dating from the 18th century that was originally built to operate logging in the valleys. This location is an angling paradise. Access is from Fréchendech – from the top of Sentein via a good hiking track passing through a lovely beach grove that hangs above the channel. There is accommodation and respite at the refuge d'Araing open from 15th May through 1st October. Tel, 0561967373 / 0561967727, there is room for 52 anglers. Capacity in winter is 6 places. For more information go to the barrages des Pyrénées website. http://www.vallees-ax.com/index_hiver_fr.html

Couserans at Riberot

Etang Rond du Ribèrot: 2320 m above sea level is a beautiful natural lake covering 7 ha. A rock face forming a small cirque surrounds it. It is perfectly round and at the bottom a small waterfall descends from the Long pond, it's very nice. The lake is situated in the centre of a nature reserve; anglers can normally spot chevraies d'isard – mountain goats, marmots, golden eagle, gypaète barbu – bearded vulture. This pond is ideal for the observation of the fauna and the flora of the réserve du Mont Valier.

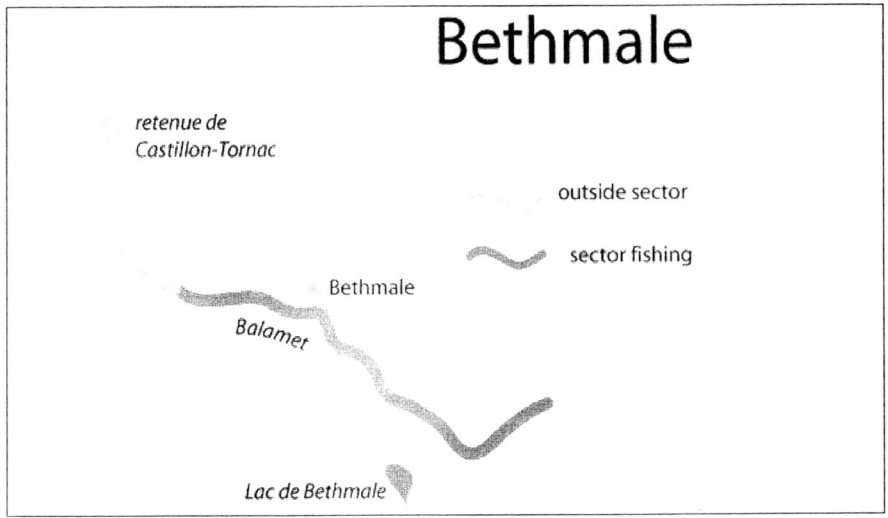

A legend is related with this pool. It is about the shepherd Mount Ner, who kept his herd on the banks of the lake, it transformed him, its dogs and its sheep into rocks because he refused to help a man who had lost his way here.

Area controlled by local angling club called Les Riverains du Balamet based in Bethmale.

Contact: Patrice Vasset Tel, +33 (0) 561029417

Areas to fish include the streams and lakes in the vallée de Bethmale Balamet Riverin vicinity of Bethmale, fish from the digue de lac de Bethmale - dyke downstream to the road from Mournt to Nert.

Purchase your angling licence from Mme Galey at Samortein in Bethmale Tel, +33 (0) 561961422.

Lakes to fish

Lac de Bethmale: 1074 m above sea level 1 ha. bt, tac, sdf The legend tells that a wicked witch lived hidden by Lake Bethmale a very a long time ago. Every day, she created misery among the inhabitants of the local village. One day angry villagers climbed the col de la Core with pitchforks to kill the witch. Who then to escape by jumping into the lake and swearing that the water would never dry up: so they would never find here. Since then the water is blue green all the way down and gives the lake a unique reflection.

Lac de Avès, 1.7ha, bt and gr.
Lac de Eycheille, 0.6ha, bt.
Lac de Milouga, 1.75ha, bt and sdf.
Lac de Arrouech, 2.7ha, bt and sdf
Lac de Cruzous, 1.3ha, bt.
Lac de Estagnous, 0.3ha, bt and sdf
Lac deRond, 7.4ha, bt.
Lac deLong, 8.1ha, bt.

Lac de Bethmale is classified as a parcours touristique - specifically intended for leisure anglers on holiday and is open from 30th April through 30th June on Saturday, Sunday and public holidays. From 1st July until the general date for close of season for 1st category waters it's open every day except Tuesday and Friday. 10 day tickets are available. Maggots are banned. One rod only is permitted.

E. The Pays d'Olmes is located at the east end of the département de l'Ariège, bordering the Aude, between the plaine de Mirepoix and the Massif de Tabe - Pic St Barthélémy, 2368 mabove sea level where the station des Monts d'Olmes – ski resort and some high altitude lakes are located.

The étangs de Fage Belle are 2 small lakes 1,2 ha and 0,5 ha situated above the station des Monts d'Olmes by the foot of the pic Galinat 2115 m above sea level. The two lakes opened in 2006 on Wednesday, Saturday, Sunday and public holidays natural baits only allowed.

Hospitalet

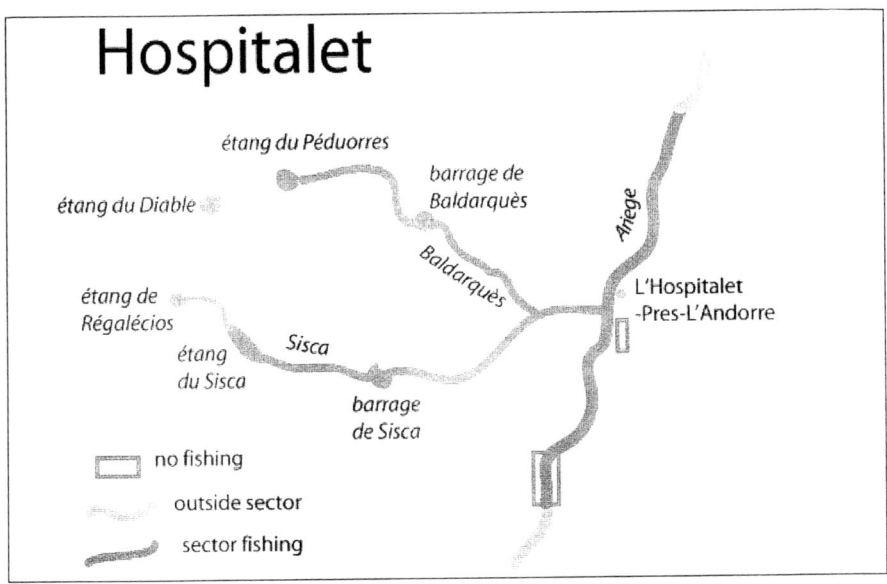

Area controlled by local angling club called Societe de Pêche de l'Hospitalet based at l'Hospitalet. Contact Philippe Rousset Tel, 0561052171 / 05610520.04. Purchase your angling licence from this organisation.

Areas to fish include the Ariège River from its confluence with the ruisseau des bésines to the barrage Verdié. And the ruisseau des Bésines, du Sisca and du baldarqués.

Réserves de pêche: ruisseau de la Gare et de la Mine – Commune and ruisseaux pépinière.

Carte complete – annual angling licence costs €62.5, carte vacances - €30, carte jeune – under 16's - €24, under 12's - €2.

Local lakes

Etang du Sisca, (4.3ha) 2187 m above sea level, 3 hours travelling time from l'Hospitalet, it contains trf, tac, cris, sdf.

Barrage du Baldarqués, (0.54ha) 1970 m above sea level, 1 ½ hours travelling time, it contains trf, tac, cris, sdf.

Etang du Pédourés, (5.5ha) 2105 m above sea level, 2 ½ hours travelling time, it contains trf, tac, cris, sdf.

The étang du Diable 1971 m above sea level, 3,5 ha, contains trf, tac, cris, sdf. was previously known as the Etang du Males. The legend says that if a stone there is thrown into the water, half an hour later the lake starts to bubble, with sulphuric eruptions, then storms, and lightning. The path ascends along a mêne – deer track to 2 small lakes, one is surrounded by a grass bank, one can then ascend the pass between Soularac and St Barthelemy if the weather is good, the view is worth the effort, Toulouse can be easily spotted, from this elevated point, as well as all of the vallée d'Olmes with the lac de Montbel, Montcalm and so on. This peak is very dangerous because of fog and lightning is especially attracted to the massif de Tabe or Tabor although the rain falls elsewhere. 2 ½ hours travelling time.

Barrage du Sisca, (0.4ha), 2025 m above sea level, 1 hour 50 minutes travelling time, it contains trf.

Etangs de Régalécios, both 1st and 2nd category, (0.25ha) 2310 m above sea level,. 3 hours 15 minutes travelling time, they contain trf, sdf.

Accommodation in l'Hospitalet: Camping municipal Tel, 0561052110. Gîtes d'étapes Tel, 0561052314. Hôtel Restaurant du Puymorens Tel, 0561052003.

There is an anglers' hostel / refuge called Les Tutes d'Ariège a **** campsite situated by the river bank it's called Le Pré Lombard.

F. The vallée d'Orlu next to d'Ax les Thermes is known to most by the national Réserve nationale de faune d'Orlu - 4150 hectares of high-mountain from 930 m to 2,765 m above sea level, created in 1947, it is the vallée de L'Oriège. There are lots of lakes of which the étang de Naguilles 81 ha and étangs d'en Beys situated by the foot of the pic de l'étang Faury 2702 m above sea level. The refuge gardé d'En Beys – anglers' hostel 1950 m above sea level, is situated in the middle of the reserve, in summer it can be reached after a three-hour walk. The reserve is teeming with nature including isards, marmotes, grouse, vultures, golden eagles and bearded vultures.

Orlu

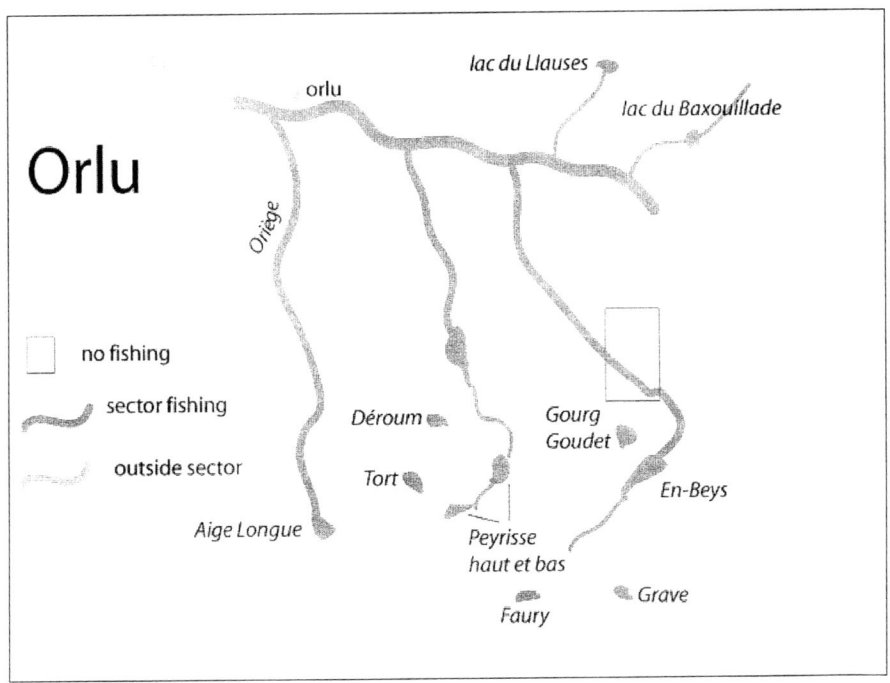

Area controlled by local angling club called Societe de Pêche de Orlu based based at Orlu, they can be contacted through Antoine Martuchou Tel, 0561643284. Angling licences are available from this contact.

Places to fish: Oriège River from the lac d'Orgeix to the pont de Caralp and its tributaries. Brown trout.

Réserves de pêche: a. Oriège River – around Orlu. Fish from the Pas de Balussières – pass, until the first refuge – angler's hut located on the upstream stretch of the Oriège River at la Jasse d'en Gaudou.

b. Ruisseau source des forges, situated in vicinity of Orlu. Fish from 200m upstream of the confluence with the Oriège River: to the confluence with the Oriège River.

Local lakes

Aigue Longue (4.5ha), 2076m a.s.l. 3 ½ hours travelling time from Orlu, trf, sdf.

Baxouillade (1.2ha), 2249m a.s.l. 4 hours away, trf
Déroum (5.7ha), 2133m a.s.l. 4 hours away, trf
En-Beys (16ha), 1954m a.s.l. 3 hours away, trf, cri
Faury (2.4ha), 2312m a.s.l. 5 hours away, trf
Gourg Gouadet (1.7ha), 1943m a.s.l. 3 ¼ hours's away, trf
Graves Bas (1.6ha), 2229m a.s.l. 4 ½ hours away, trf
La Couillade (1ha), 1975m a.s.l. 3 ¼ hours away, trf
Llauses (0.45ha), 1995m a.s.l. 1 ½ hours away, trf

The étang de Naguilles 1855m above sea level 81 ha. obl, cri. The dam was constructed between 1957 and 1959 and brought into service in 1961. This lake existed well before the dam, and was full of fish, just like the brook upstream that flows down from Peyrisses. 3 hours away.

Perisse Bas – lower lake (8ha), 2227 m above sea level 5 ½ hours away, trf, sdf
Perisse haut – upper lake (0.3ha), 2234 m above sea level 4 hours away, trf
Tort (3.8ha), 2216 m above sea level 4 ½ hours away, sdf

Outstanding places to fish: a. Oriège River, fish from the pont de Caralp – upstream limit downstream to the place des Abattuts where the maison des loups - house is situated, downstream limit.b. Ruisseau de la vallée d'Orgeix, in its totality. Officially these stretches are reserved for anglers who live in orlu, but a bit of persuasion should do the trick.

Accommodation: Relais Montagnard, Orlu Tel, 0561646188.

G. Located the Eastern extreme part of the Pyrenees Ariégeoises, the **Pays du Donezan** - canton de Quérigut is an area surrounded by a great number of peaks of from 2300 m to2800 m above sea level. It is an island of greenery: the forest covers more than half the area and it supports a rich diversity of flora and fauna. There are mountain lakes and many streams that attract anglers. In winter the ski resort of Mijanes attracts many visitors and accessible on foot from the station are the popular attraction called the forges à la catalane woman.
The étang de Laurenti 1936 m above sea level 6 ha, is located in a cirque of pastures surrounded by very steep slopes and high peaks: the Roc Blanc 2543 m above sea level the pic de Baxouillade 2544 m above sea level. it gets plenty of water. There are brown trout in the stream that

flows out of the lake at the bottom of the escarpment where the fish feed on insect larvae and aquatic plants thrive. There are tree lines banks.

The barrage de Noubals 1229 m above sea level 16 ha is a lake holding 2 million m3 with splendid views of the Roc Blanc and a scene that offers a kaleidoscope of colours throughout the changing seasons.

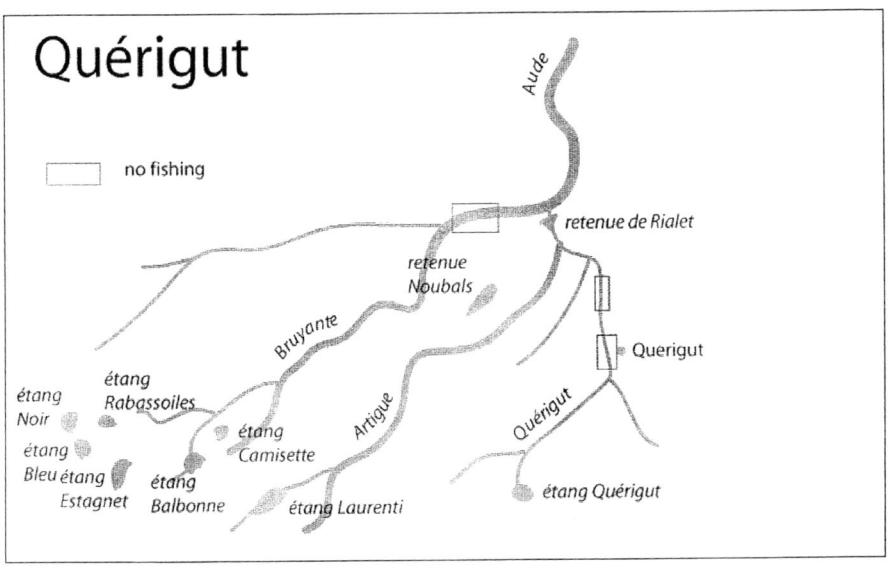

Area controlled by local angling club called Canton de Quérigut based at Quérigut contact Jean-François Sanche Tel, 0468204536.

Angling licence can be purchased at: Alimentation Services du Donezan, Quérigut Tel, 0568204532.

Places to fish: Aude, Bruyante, Laurenti, Quérigut Rivers, and their tributaries. Brown trout.

Réserves de pêche: réserve Fédéral - plan d'eau de Noubals, fishing permitted on a third of the lake at its tail end, look out for notice boards on site for guidance.

Bruyante River: crossing through towns of Rouze and Muanes. Look out for signposting upstream and downstream limits to the stretches.

Quérigu River in vicinity of Lepla. Fish from the Pont de l' ancienne filature – mill downstream to the Station d'épuration – water treatment plant

Quérigut River at Quérigut, fish from the Garage Ponts et Chaussées downstream to the pont du Moulin.

Local lakes – all of them contain brown trout

Etang de Balbonne (2.6ha), 1891 m above sea level 1 hour's drive from Quérigut
Etang de la Camisette (0.3ha), 2142 m above sea level 2 hours away
Etang de l'Estagnet (1.25ha), 1987 m above sea level 1 ½ hours away
Etang de Laurenti (6.5ha), 1936 m above sea level 1 ½ hours away

The étang de Quérigut 1876 m above sea level 3 ha. Is located in the middle of a pine forest on a plateau situated immediately to the north west of an escarpment buttress by the pic Ginébra. The lake has supported omble chevalier. It is a tree lined lake. 1 hour away.

Etang du Rabassoles Bas – lower lake (6.6ha), 1851 m above sea level 1 hour away
Etang Rabassoles Bleu (4.4ha), 1920 m above sea level 1 ½ hours away
Etang Rabassoles Noir (2.7ha), 1970 m above sea level 1 hour 50 minutes away

Accommodation: Camping La Pradaille, Lepla Tel, 0468.204914
Hôtel Restaurant Relais de Pailhères, Mijanes Tel, 0468204697.
Hôtel Restaurant Le Donezan, Quérigut Tel, 0468204240.
Les Soulades, Lepla Tel, 0468204800.

Area controlled by local angling club called la Truite Sigueroise based at Siguer, contact Jean Antoniutti Tel, 0561058743 / 0561051316.

Angling licences can be obtained from Robert Moreau in Sigeur Tel, 0561055351.

Places to fish, all locations support brown trout: Siguer River upstream of Laramade and its tributaries. The ruisseau du Gnioure.

Réserves de Pêche

Canal de la scierie – fishable along its whole course.
Ruisseau le Siguer in vicinity of Siguer, fish from the bridge at exit to Siguer - or la Palanque. Downstream to the barrage de EDF – water authority dam: in the village.

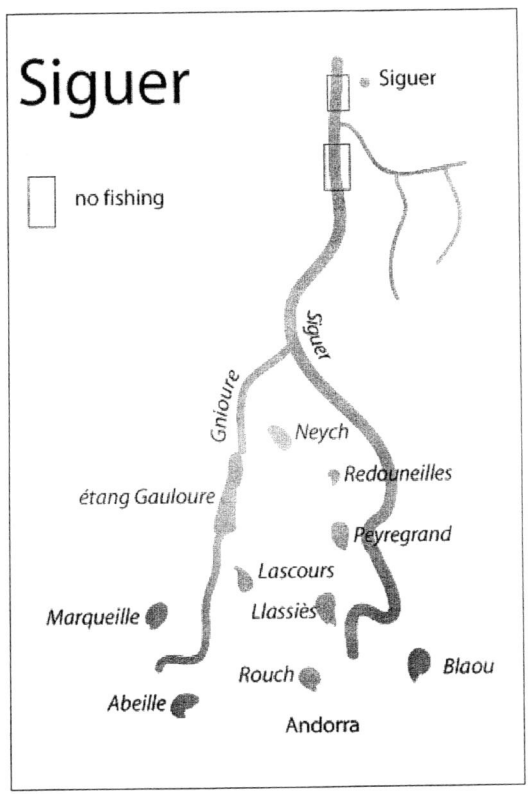

Prade River in vicinity of Sigeur, fish from its source downstream to the confluence with the Sigeur River.
Local lakes

Abeille (1.3ha), 2361m a.s.l. 5 ½ hours drive from Sigeur, trf
Blaou (16.5ha), 2345m a.s.l. 6 hours away, trf, sdf, cris
Gnioure (85ha), 1832m a.s.l. 3 ½ hours away, trf, tac, obl, cris
Goueille (3.7ha), 2393m a.s.l. 5 ½ hours away, trf
Lascours- two lakes (2.4ha), 2209m a.s.l. 4 ½ hours away, trf
Llassiès – four lakes (2.4ha), 2386m a.s.l. 6 hours away, trf

Marqueille (1.2ha), 2431m a.s.l. 5 hours away, trf
Monescur (0.3ha), 1927m a.s.l. 3 hours away, trf
Peyregrand (2.9ha), 1898m a.s.l. 3 ½ hours away, trf sdf
Rouch (4.3ha), 2549m a.s.l. 6 hours away, obl

Outstanding places to fish in this area

Upstream of the réserve, for a 2.5 km stretch until the passerelle de l'ancienne école de la Prade – old school footbridge, this parcours de pêche – river stretch is reserved for residents of Siguer, however a little friendly persuasion will achieve results. The étangs de Neych and Redouneilles: visitors can fish these lakes.

Reservoirs in Ariège

The Ariège département has twelve dams, 11 of which are used in the production of hydroelectric power by the EDF. Their interest lies in the factthat they offer good destinations for walking routes.

The dams are: Araing, Castillon s/Lez, Garrabet, Gnioure, Goulours , Izourt, Lanoux , Laparan, Naguilhes, Pla de Soulcem, Riete, L'artigue.

Accessible: after the étang d'Izourt. The refuge Fourcat – anglers hostel is the highest in Ariège and surrounded by the Pics de Tristagne 2870 m above sea level and Malcaras 2865 m above sea level It can sleep 45 people and is open from July 1st through 15th September. On weekends June through September reservation are needed Tel, 0561654315 bailiffs is Yan Dubourg Tel, 0561031565.

A local angling club affiliated to the AAPPMA is called La Truite Appameenne. It controls parts of the Ariège river depicted on the regional map at the start of this chapter. The club's president is called Bernard Bonnet Tel, +33 (0) 561673348. The areas to fish are: the Ariège River situated downstream of the track from Saint-Jean de Verges to Crampagna. The Ariège River situated upstream and downstream of Pamiers. The Hers River situated downstream of Rieucros.

In addition the fishing club maintains réserves de pêche – fishing reserves on the Ariège River (canal de Guilhot) situated near the towns of Rieux de Pelleport and Benagues, the stretch is 1.2 km long. Fish from: the vannes - sluice gates at entrance of the canal coming from the centrale de Guilhot - power station until 50 m downstream of l'usine de Guilhot – factory.

On Ariège River: canal de Crampagna situated by town of Crampagna fish along a 450 m stretch. Fish from: the sluice gate at entrance to the canal coming from the centrale de Crampagna until 50 m downstream of l'ursine de Crampagna - factory.

Ariège River: (canal de Pébernat) by Pamiers and Bonnac. Fish from the sluice gate holding the water of the EDF canal de Pébernat until the confluence with the Ariège River.

Ruisseau de Lafargue near Bonnac. Fishing permitted all around Bonnac.

Canaux de la ville de Pamiers. Fish along its course except for the stretch between the pont de l'Office de Tourisme: downstream to the pont de Ste-Hélène.

Purchase your **angling licence** in Pamiers at: Intersport Tel, +33 (0) 561 684200 and Grandeur Nature situated in Saint-Jean du Falga Tel, +33 (0) 561670725.

Day tickets for the parcours de pêche – fishing resrve cost €2 for under anglers under twelve. Contact: Office de Tourisme Tel, +33 (0) 561675252.

Parcours Touristiques de Pêche - angling venues for those on holiday

Two parcours touristiques are present in this départment, they are regularly stocked with trout and day tickets are available locally. They are maintained as easy places to fish and catches are nearly guaranteed but not totally guaranteed, that would be called catching fish not fishing. Access **facilities for anglers with restricted mobility** are provided.

Lac de Bethmale: 1074 m above sea level Directions: from Saint-Girons, take the D 618 towards Castillon en Couserans as far as Bordes sur Lez, where you take a left for theD 7 ascending the vallée de Bethmale. The lake is found after 10 km. Another route exists via Seiux then the col de la Core.

The lake is open from 29th April through 17th September. Until 30th June fishing is only allowed on Weekends and public holidays. After July 1st fishing is every day except Tuesday and Friday.

Day tickets cost €10 for those anglers in procession of a licence, otherwise cost is €13. **Day tickets** are available from: Monsieur Patrice Vasset Tel, 0561029417, Monsieur Joseph Domenc Tel, 05619675 50, Madame Galey Tel, 0561961422.

Etang de Lers: 1274 m above sea level Directions: from Saint-Girons, take the D 618 until the tunnel de Kercabanac then until Massat, then the D 18 towards Le Port, 9 km further on is the lake.

Another route: from Saint-Girons, take the D 618 until the tunnel de Kercabanac, then the D 32 towards Oustas far as Aulus les Bains. Follow the sign - Port de Lers where is situated the lake after a 7km climb up the pass. This route from Tarascon, Vicdessos and Suc et Sentenac.

The lake is open from 3rd June until 17th September everyday. Day tickets cost €11 with an angling licence otherwise the cost is €14. Contact M. Galy Tel, 0561049113.

Parcours de Pêche – catch and release fly-fishing stretches

The Fédération de Pêche – national angling body and the AAPPMA de l'Ariège have set aside angling locations specifically for trout anglers, all areas are signposted. Barbless hooks must be used.

On two plans d'eau de Fage Belle, spinning lures and fly-fishing are allowed. The lakes are open from 25th May through 17th September on Wednesday, Weekends and public holidays. Day tickets are available locally. Try bars and newsagents.

On the Garbet River situated at Erce and Ariège River situated at Luzenac all methods of fishing are allowed. Fly-fishing only on the Ariège River situated at Tarascon-sur-Ariège, Arac River situated at

Biert, Salat River situated at Saint Girons. On the Touyre River at Régat and Arize River found towards Mas d'Azil – natural baits are also allowed.

Locations to fish for trout for anglers with restricted mobility

In Ariège département, there are 7 trout fishing venues with **facilities for anglers with restricted mobility** located within ½ hour and ¾ hour from Tarascon. There are two other locations for anglers with restricted mobility to fish in Couserans at the étang de Bethmale, and the Bouigane River found at Aucazein. And two more facilities in the Pays d'Olmes: the Touyre River at Lavelanet, and the Hers River at Bélesta. Since 2004 facilities for anglers with restricted mobility have also been in place at the étang de Lers, Vicdessos River at Auzat and the Roziès River at Montégut-Plantaurel.

Fly-Fishing guides – provide tuition for novices

Robert Menquet based at Couserans, fly-fishing expert, Boussan 09320 Soulan Tel, 0561.968889 or 0682974077.

Stéphane Villaine, based at Couserans, specialises in fly-fishing for trout and grayling, Rue du Pont 09200 Moulis Tel, 0680388000. http://www.guidemouche.com/ email: stephane.villaine@wanadoo.fr

Gérald Nicoine, based at Pêche Sportive in Kercorb, an expert in fishing for silure- Wels catfish, pike and perch at the lac de Montbel including from his boat, Hameau les Bernots 11260 Saint-Jean de Paracol Tel, 0468742208 or 0678956257.

Thibault Gayraud, based in the Haute Ariège, specialises in fly-fishing for brown and rainbow trout and grayling, 04, quartier Loum 09250 Luzenac Tel, 0670937411. http://pyreneespeche.free.fr

Laurent Chapeyrou is based in the Haute Ariège and is an expert guide for the surrounding mountain lakes. He specialises in fly-fishing – alternative-fishing methods may be used, for brown and rainbow trout, omble de fountaine and omble chevalier. 3 rue de la Mauve 09400 Tarascon-sur-Ariège Tel, 0561647426 or 0673796880.

http://laurent.chapeyrou.chez-alice.fr/   Email: l.chapeyrou@viola.fr
Laurent can also take you on excursions farther a field into Spain. He speaks English, Catalan and Spanish. Visit Laurent's website at: http://laurent.chapeyrou.chez.tiscali.fr/

Écoles des Pêche – fishing schools

Ecole de Saint-Girons. Open every Wednesday from 20th April through 25th June from 4-6pm. Contact M. Castellot Tel, 0561963004 or 0561966382.

Ecole de Mazères. Open all through the year on Wednesday from 9.30-11.30 a.m. Contact: M. Ville Tel, 0561697515 or 0683516873, M. Charrie Tel, 0561694482 or M. Berge Tel, 0561694238.

Local angling clubs

Club Mouche du Pays d'Olmes, contact: Mr. Pierre Ville, 64 rue du Foulon 09100 PamiersTel, 0561697515.

Club Mouche du Couserans, contact: Mr. Thierry Valero, chemin de la Peyrade 09300 Belesta.

Club Mouche de la Vallée de l'Ariège, contact: Mr. André Souque, 43 avenue du Maréchal Foch 09200 Saint Girons Tel, 0561662899.

www.lacsdespyrenees.com website is well worth a visit, it contains excellent photography for all the mountain lakes listed under the Ariège chapter and for neighbouring départements along the Pyrenees and lakes on the Spanish side. Photographs displayed on this website depict fish species found in this region.
Many of the Spanish mountain lakes and rivers are included in my book called Fly-Fishing in Northern Spain, details for obtaining a copy are provided at the end of this book or go to my website www.spainfishing.com.

Fish species found in the Pyrenees lakes and rivers – the English name is followed by the French and the scientific name in italics.

Brown trout, truite fario, *Salmo trutta fario*. Average length: 20-35 cm; maximum: 1 m Average weight: 150-400 G; maximum: more than 7 kg Lifespan: 6 to 13 years. An indigenous fish species the brown trout of natural stock is the commonest fish found in the Pyrenean lakes and it is the only one that was present before stocking with fish that started about 1930. its livery varies from black, yellow or brown with red spots. The trout caught in deeper water have a clearer livery that often resembles rainbow trout it breeds every three years.

Arctic Charr, Omble Chevalier or Omble Arctique, *Salvelinus alpinus alpinus* Average length: 20 to 30 cm; maximum: 45 to 50 cm. Average weight in the Pyrenees: 250-400 G; maximum: 2 kg Lifespan: 10-20 years. Omble Chevalier is a native fish species originally from the Alps. It was introduced into the Pyrenees about 1936. The omble chevalier is similar to the brown trout but it has smaller scales – in excess of 200 scales on each flank. Livery varies according to sex and time of year.

At the time of the reproduction, the omble has bright colours, in particular on the belly marked in red. The omble is king of large alpine lakes. The omble knight is a primarily lake fish, it thrives in deep water that is cold and is well oxygenated at a depth between 30 and 70 meters. The omble chevalier eats remains of plants, small molluscs, larvae of insects, small shellfish and young fish. It reaches sexual maturity between 4 and 5 years for the male and from 5 to 10 years for the female. Spawning takes place from November to January, in general, on rock beds more than 60m deep. The eggs incubate from 3 to 4 months; because of the low temperature of water the development of the juvenile people ombles is very slow. Since the 1980's, a small fish farm located in the Pyrenees has operated to breed these fish in water temperature less than 10 centigrade all year round.

American Brook charr or speckled trout, Omble de Fontaine, *Salvelinus fontinalis*, commonly called Saumon de Fontaine, truite mouchetée, truite saumonée, truite rouge. Introduced fish species. Average length: 20 - 25 cm; maximum: 35-40 cm Average weight in the Pyrenees: 250-400 G; maximum: 1 kg Lifespan: 5 to 7 years. Omble de Fontaine or Salmon of Fountain were introduced in Frnace from

North America, the name Omble de Fontaine was created in France where this fish initially bred well in fish farms fed by natural springs.

Its introduction into the Pyrenees goes back to 1930 where it is more often called the Saumon de Fountaine. It's an endemic species of the eastern seaboard of North America where it is called mouchetée trout or brook trout, it has been introduced everywhere into the world. In Canada, it as widespread in inland waters as well as on the coast, the fresh water populations seek clean water in temperatures lower than 20°C in clear brooks, rivers and well-oxygenated lakes.

It is similar to the brown trout. The mouth is largely split, the jawbone exceeding the posterior edge of the eye. The end of the caudal fin is indented a little. Its livery is often very bright, especially during spawning. The back and the sides are green-blue-ish, they display pale, vermiculated spots. On the flanks are red spots. The belly is pink.

Omble de Fountaine are carnivorous. Its diet is varied, including worms, shellfish, insects, spiders, molluscs, frogs and fish. The adults eat sometimes eggs or young fish of their own species and lifespan seldom exceeds 12 years in its natural environment.

It is a gregarious fish often found in schools but its size remains modest in the Pyrenees, between 20 and 30cm. According to the studies made in Canada the Omble de Fountaine (if it manages to spawn in mountain lakes: there is little information available on this subject) spawning takes place in late summer or early autumn. Spawning generally takes place on gravel beds, in shallower water, in upstream rivers. It may also occur on the gravel shallow waters of lakes, where there is a spring and a moderate current – a possibility in some mountain lakes.

American Lake charr, Cristivomer, *Salvelinus namaycush*, commonly called Touladi or Omble du Canada; it is an introduced species. Average length: 35 - 40 cm maximum: 1,10m. Average weight in the Pyrenees: 600G maximum: 10 kg Lifespan: in excess of 20 years.

Cristivomer were introduced into the Pyrenees in about 1956. Originating in Canada where it is more often called touladi or grey trout, it can reach in that country 1,20 m length and more than 30 kg. A grey trout of 30 kg was taken in Great Bear Lake in 1991, in the Territories of the North West in Canada. A Grey of 46.3 kg was caught in a net in the lake at Athabasca in Saskatchewan in 1961. The French national record for the cristivomer is 8.110 kg, caught in 1992 in the département of Hautes-Pyrénées.

The cristivomer has a defense mechanism where it bangs its head on the bottom and can give the angler a terrific fight. The cristivomer presents the general characteristics of a char. It has a pointed head its mouth is largely split and the end of the jawbone exceeding the posterior edge of the eye.

The name of cristivomer comes from the teeth of its palate that are laid out in form of cross. Its colouring is variable according to the season and its physiological state, the livery is often mainly grey with many spots covering all of the body, being vermiculated on the back and the dorsal fin. In larger lakes its livery can turn completely silver.

This species is gregarious but found more often in smaller groups than large schools. Older specimens are loners. During colder months the fish stay close to the surface, as the water warms they drop down during the summer to well oxygenated and coldwater.

It is wary of light but at night comes up to the surface. It reproduces in October-November, when the temperature of water becomes lower than 5°C.

The cristivomer reproduces only from 6 or 7 years old but it can exceed 20 years in age. It is a fish which hybrids naturally with others salmonidés, some hybrids are known as Splake - omble de fontaine mâle and cristivomer female. Its diet consists of insects, molluscs and shellfish. But it also attacks its own young.

Rainbow trout, Truite Arc en Ciel, *Oncorhynchus mykiss*, introduced species. Average length: 20 - 30cm; maximum: 70cm. Average weight in the Pyrenees: 300 - 400G; maximum: 3 to 5 kg Lifespan: 8 to 9 years.   Originally from North America, the rainbow trout is the trout species that breeds best in fish farms, it is a great fighter and grows fast.

It reproduces in some lakes located in the Pyrénées Orientales e.g. Barrages des Bouillouses, Lanoux and Matemale. But only rarely: in the lakes of the Pyrénées Occidentales. Except for an isolated example in the Réserve Naturelle de l'Estibère in the Vallée d'Aure at lac de l'Ours, however angling is not allowed in this small valley. For some years trout stocks have originated from the Pyrénées Orientales, especially brown trout from the Vallée de Luchon.

The rainbow trout has a spindle-shaped body. Its head is relatively small, its mouth is split a little, the jawbone not exceeding the outside edge of the eye. The body displays on the flank a characteristic iridescent band. The dorsal fins and anal present black punctuations those are absent in brown trout. The general colouring of the body is very variable according to the types of environment and physiological state. The rainbow trout has hearty appetite and feeds at all depths.

Hybrids. Splake: Salvelinus namaycush – cristivomer, female and Salvelinus fontinalis - omble de fontaine, male. Introduced at the beginning into the great Canadian lakes to replace Omble the victim of the marine lamprey. A test was carried out in a Pyrénéen lake at very high altitude – 2700 m above sea level on Splakes introduced in 1992, the studie's findings proved inconclusive on the question of naturalization, too premature for results but its growth rate in the test lake area was lower than that of the comparable Omble de Fountaine.

http://www.state.me.us/ifw/fishing/fishidentification/splake.htm

Other hybrids: Truite Mulak - Omble chevalier female + omble de fontaine. Truite Léopard – brown trout + rainbow trout. Truites tigrées have been bread at a private fish farm in Baudéan (65).

MORE TITLES IN EUROPEAN ANGLING SERIES

The purchase price for each title is £10 plus £1 p+p. Ad another £1 per title: when ordering from Europe. Why not buy two titles for £18 including p+p. To find out more or order a copy, telephone (+44) 01708 764 696. E-mail: philippembroke007@hotmail.com
Or visit: www.spainfishing.com

All my fishing guidebooks can be purchased on my website: www.spainfishing.com

My first volume curently available is called **The Essential Guide to Coarse Fishing in Spain**. ISBN – 8489954496 Reviewed by the Angling Times in October 2003, they said...

"This book contains excellent information on 130 popular angling locations, including the all the Costa regions and Canary Islands. Plus the Guadiana and Tajo Rivers located in Extremadura and northern Spain's Duero River. This 200 pages book deals with top fishery locations, obtaining licences, and also offers best fishing methods.

My second book title also available is called Pesca a Cana, **Angling in Portugal**. The Angler's Mail said in their **** star review 2004...

"Brilliant advice for coarse, game and sea fishing all over Portugal, expert tips on fishing favourite waters."

My third title "**Pêche Français I, Coarse Angling in France Volume I**" ISBN- 095469242X. Reviewed by the Angler's Mail in August 2004, they write,"The book concentrates on the exact information you want from this type of guide and covers those rivers and lakes that can be fished simply by buying a local fishing licence."

My fourth title "**Pêche Français II, Coarse Angling in France Volume II.**" ISBN – 0954692489.Covers the rivers Marne, Yonne, Seine and Yonne situated east of Paris plus the regions of Gironde in southwest France and Haute-Vienne in Limoges.

My fifth title "**Pescando a Mosca – Fly fishing in Spain**" ISBN- 0954692438 is 156 pages in length and covers fishing for salmon and trout in the Asturias, Castilla and León, Catalunya, València, Alicante, Murcia, Almería, Málaga, Cádiz, Seville and Granada.

There are three more titles that cover fly-fishing in Spain's individual regions in greater depth, they are: **Fly-Fishing in Asturias** ISBN – 09546924-5-4 – great for salmon, sea trout and trout. **Fly-Fishing in Galica** ISBN – 0-9546924-4-6 – great for sea trout, trout and Black bass. **Fly-Fishing in Northern Spain** ISBN – 0-9546924-6-2, great for trout, Hucho freshwater salmon and large pike in León, Salamanca, Zamora, La Rioja, Navarra and Catalyuna - Pyrenees.

CONCLUSION

Have a great time fly-fishing in France. Some fantastic game fishing awaits you in rivers and lakes surrounded by fantastic scenery. Of course France is also famous for excellent food and wine.

Further reading

Aphrodite's Carp – John Langridge, Medlar Press ISBN – 1899600442
Freshwater Fish of Britain and Europe – Peter S. Maitland, Hamlyn, ISBN – 0 600 59690 7

Glossary 1 - Salmon conservation organisations in France

SOS Loire Vivante
8, rue Crozatier
43000 LE PUY
Tél. 04 71 05 57 88
Fax 04 71 02 60 99
e mail: sosloirevivante@rivernet.org

Association Protectrice du Saumon (APS)
Chemin des Coustilles
6340 LE BREUIL-SUR-COUZE
Président: Paul Brunet.

Club Mouche Saumon Allier (CMSA)
12, rue de l'Ouradou
63000 CLERMONT-FERRAND
Président: François Grebot

Association Protectrice du Saumon de Souche Allier (APSSA)
Lotissement La Chênaie
03 700 BELLERIVE-SUR-ALLIER
Président : M.CHAVAILLON